Pull the other one!

Roger Evans

Britain's Favourite Dairy Farmer

MERLIN UNWIN BOOKS

First published in Great Britain by Merlin Unwin Books Ltd, 2018

Merlin Unwin Books Ltd
Palmers House
7 Corve Street
Ludlow
Shropshire SY8 1DB
U.K.

www.merlinunwin.co.uk

The author asserts his moral right to be identified with this work.

ISBN 978-1-910723-80-7

Typeset in 11 point Bembo by Merlin Unwin Books
Printed by TJ International Ltd, Padstow, Cornwall

9 January 2016

There have been times in my life when topics for me to write were queuing up, clamouring for attention. In some sort of chronological order, firstly there was Mert, my sheepdog. His exploits, terrorising ramblers, joggers and anyone else who was close at hand, became legendary. Then, by the simple expedient of wanting a few hens and a cockerel scratching about the yard, we got Neville the cockerel, who provided endless interest and who was so ferocious that he made Mert look like a pussycat. Neville went inside a fox about three years ago but I still get people coming on the yard and winding their windows down and asking if it safe to get out or whether that blankety cockerel is still about. Seamlessly, no sooner had Neville gone than we had the turkeys. They took the danger level on our yard up to terrorist degree until I had to get rid of them, for everyone's safety, not least my own.

So what's next? I cast my mind about for further challenges. I've got the Alpine bell on a cow, which delights and annoys people in equal measure, but is that enough? No, it's not really, I have a reputation to keep up. Then news comes in that there is a possibility of acquiring two donkeys. It's a longish story but it seems that someone put the donkeys in someone's field 12 months ago and they couldn't be contacted to fetch them back when the field was no longer available. So I was asked if I'd home them. They were two old Jack donkeys, 12 and 14, and I said yes. This was a good thing. Top of my wife's wish list is a corgi puppy, but there's no way we can afford one. I've tried to locate a rescue one without success. But second on her wish list is a donkey. Two donkeys are even better. One could be for her Christmas present and the other for her birthday next August.

But life can be a let-down. I said yes to the donkeys on Wednesday, got a nice dry shed ready for them on Thursday, but on Friday the real owner turned up out of the blue and took them away. So for two days I thought that I had two donkeys and I'd

1

never even seen them! Have you ever seen a dead donkey? An old man who used to work for me often used to say, 'Not many have seen a dead donkey.' He clearly thought that seeing one was some sort of accolade. I have to admit I've never seen one. He had seen one when he was a boy and he thought that having seen one was an important milestone in his life. The one he'd seen was in a village a few miles away. He reckoned it had been left unburied for ten days, just so folks could have a chance to see it. And it was a chance that they took, in their hundreds. He reckoned that people came for miles around in pony traps and on their bikes. 'Not many folks have seen a dead donkey,' he said, 'but I saw it twice.' And he left to carry on with the hedge he was laying, and there was a swagger of pride about him, his body language was very positive. I never quite worked out why seeing a dead donkey was so important in people's lives. I asked him once and he looked at me scornfully and did not dignify my question with a reply. Two old Jack donkeys would have been good. I bet they would have made one hell of a noise.

★★★

Christmas, long gone as it is, still leaves a feeling of disappointment. I had seriously thought that my grandchildren would have clubbed together and bought me an illuminated taxi sign to put on the roof of my car. A meter to cost journeys would have been nice as well.

16 JANUARY 2016

I've never considered myself to be an envious person. But today I find that I envy the keeper. Because the land is so wet, I have to confine my trips around the farm to where I can go by 4x4 on the tracks. The keeper has a quad bike that will take him everywhere. We've never had a quad bike, we buy old 4x4 trucks, so he tells me, the keeper, that there are a pair of curlews about. I've not seen any curlews taking to flight for years. A pair of curlews taking to flight at dawn and the plaintive cry the make, is one of the most beautiful sounds devised by nature. Twenty or thirty years ago, it was a sound I would hear most days as I called the cows for morning milking and my shouts had disturbed them. So let's hope that the pair breed, let's hope they stay around here and let's hope that even if I don't see them, I hear them. But the keeper isn't finished yet. 'I was on your side field above the wood at dusk one night and there were about 70 woodcock out there feeding.' They were shooting last Saturday and I ask him, warily, if the woodcock were about then. Some shooters get very excited if there are woodcock about and see shooting one as some sort of accolade. I've never shot at one, why would you feel the need to shoot such a lovely small bird that has flown so far just to be here?

The keeper tells me that it has been forbidden to shoot at woodcock on this shoot for years and years. That's good news, let's see if there's any more. 'What about hares?' He tells me that he put a 'stop' at the top of one wood. (A stop is a beater placed to prevent pheasants escaping on foot in order to avoid being driven over guns.) That stop has seen 14 hares slip away through a gap in the fence. He himself had seen a similar number go out of a different wood. So it's a good news day. Don't feel quite so envious of the quad bike now.

★★★

Farm cats are an interesting phenomenon. I'm always talking about balance and balance is something we try to apply to our farm cats. All our cats are wild. When we have farm assurance visits we are always asked about farm cats and I always say that they are feral. When we have farm assurance visits, especially to the poultry, we have to produce invoice evidence that we have regular visits from a rodent control firm, ie rat catchers. That's all very well but a resident population of healthy farm cats is the real answer. I call them feral because there's always been cats here but they are cats that have just turned up. They are mostly very wild and you can't touch them. Many years ago we would have visits from a big ferocious ginger tom cat. So for years we had all ginger cats, which I didn't like, probably because I didn't like the original tom cat. Now we seem to be into black cats and about once a year we have the most beautiful pure grey kittens born which are my favourites. Striking some sort of balance is the problem. We put milk out twice a day for the cats and we also feed them. But if you feed them too much they have more kittens and they in turn have more kittens and before you know where you are, cats are getting out of hand. Years ago I counted 50 cats, and that was just the ones I could see. So you try to minimise the feed you give them so that they catch some of the vermin! Kittens are mostly born in the spring. They are born in hidden places deep in the bowels of straw bays, so the first time that they come out into the world they are already spitting, explosive balls of fury. When there are too many they get cat flu and die so it is a sort of self-limiting population.

But in the autumn, well outside the new kitten season, there appeared in a cattle shed, four lovely little black kittens. Autumn usually heralds the start of what my old biology teacher used to call 'the inclement season'. So I decided that if these kittens were to survive, they needed a bit of extra help. I bought a big bag of kitten food and I would go and feed them every day. And they flourished. It was a bit of a chore taking their food every day, and you had to be devious because the dogs were watching you carry the food and as soon as you turned your back they would drive the kittens off and scoff it themselves. But it isn't a chore anymore. Cats are clever and as they grew they started to come to meet me, a bit further every day, so within a couple of weeks they had worked their way down to the kitchen door. And they live around the door, out of sight of the dogs, but stay in the vicinity until I've fed them.

As far as the family are concerned, they are my cats. They are all jet black and identical. I've told the family that one of them is called 'Blackie'. They reply that the cats are so alike I don't know which is which. (This is very true, but I don't admit it.) So I go to the kitchen door and call 'Blackie', and in no time at all, a Blackie appears soon to be followed by three more. For some reason this really winds the family up, which is why I persist in doing it.

23 JANUARY 2016

Time for a good catch-up with the keeper, time always well spent. He reminds of when he came across two vehicles in my fields in late summer, vehicles that contained eight hare coursers and 11 dogs. Naturally he asked them what they were doing there and they told him they had taken a wrong turning and were just turning around in order to get back on the lane. Quite bold and brazen, your hare courser, when challenged. So he watches them go and notes down the make and registration numbers of the vehicles, which details he gives to the police, and to me. One vehicle is a silver Subaru estate car. Moving on to the present day, the coursers have disappeared. What they like are large fields of stubble that they can drive their cars on and 'work' their dogs. Almost all fields are ploughed now and sown down to new crops.

The keeper is only part-time. He has a full-time job on a farm and does gamekeeping at each end of the day and at weekends. Part of his role on the farm is to do the spraying and to do spraying you have to go on courses that teach you how to do it properly and safely and you have to pass appropriate tests in order to carry on spraying and in order to keep your job. So it's all very important stuff. He tells me that there is a Facebook page dedicated to people who are qualified sprayers where they can all keep in touch with each other and where they can pass on tips. At least I think that's what he told me, I don't know how Facebook works and have no intention of finding out. Last week he went onto the Facebook sprayer site (which I thought was a bit sad, but each to his own), and a contributor had written there that he had a lot of trouble with hare coursers and people with dogs killing deer. Some of his fields were still in stubble awaiting spring sown crops and in order to keep these unwelcome people off these fields, he had found it very effective to plough all the way around the outside of a field, thus creating a five or six furrow barrier of loose soil that it was difficult to drive a vehicle over. I suppose it is a variation of the old fashioned sticky fly papers we use in our kitchen in the summer. If you get on there, it's difficult to get off. To illustrate the point, the contributor had included a photograph of a silver Subaru estate car firmly stuck on this ploughing and abandoned. My keeper says to his wife, 'That looks a lot like the Subaru that was about here in the autumn.' He goes out to his truck, fetches his diary, and behold, it is the very same vehicle. I've saved the best bit until last. Where do you think it was abandoned? Only in Kent, which is about 200 miles from here! The police were called and the Subaru hadn't been insured, taxed or MOT'd for 12 months. The farmer picked it up with his loader and took it to a scrap yard. It's quite difficult to catch hare coursers in the act. Seems that their vehicles should be the target.

★★★

I'm not Welsh speaking but there is a welsh word that I've always used. Cwtch. It means a sort of cuddle. It's a good word, it sounds like it means. You give a child some cwtch when it's fallen and hurt its knee. You can give a loved one some cwtch, though this can often lead to naughtiness. I was driving up the track the other day and there was a hare cwtched in some long grass, so I stopped for a chat. The hare tells me that most of her species have survived the hare coursers. That there's probably about 40 hares left. That the dogs the coursers use greyhound-cross sort of dogs, lurchers or long dogs, hunt by sight alone and can only catch a hare in a big open field. If it's a small field, a hare can get through a hole in a fence or a hedge so much quicker than a large dog. They can rarely catch a hare in the woods for similar reasons. Best of all is the 40 acres of fodder beet. A hare can escape down the rows and the large green leaves provide a canopy that keeps the hare out of sight. I like to think that I always put the needs of the farm first, I have to, but I never do anything that is negative to the wildlife. Turns out my 40 acres of fodder beet, which is grown for good farming reasons, is also an ideal sanctuary for persecuted hares. (By the way, the hare didn't tell me all this, it's my own appraisal – I thought that if I said the hare had told me, the story would have more credibility.)

30 JANUARY 2016

Don't think me to be a whinging farmer. But my bank manager was here last week and though he promised continued support in difficult circumstances, he had no idea why we bothered. When you are a farmer you spend a lot of time on your own, and you spend a lot of that time thinking about your farming. Because you are challenged every day by things that can go wrong, you aim all the time to do things better. It's a sort of, 'I got caught out by the weather this year, if I do it differently next year, I should be able to do it better.' Doing things better is what drives us along, and for generations, being a better farmer has been enough to make you a living. I've never made a lot of money but I've never been driven by making money. I've always enjoyed my way of life. But that is all under threat because of the fall in milk prices. We are told that there is too much milk in the world; we produce very slightly less than we did three years ago so I don't feel responsible for that. I can foresee nothing that will improve milk prices for 12 months so I thought I would try to cut some of my costs.

Cutting costs is usually the opposite of trying to do things better, but there is no choice. We sell about a million litres of milk a year, that's around average. A penny a litre is £10,000, so I thought that if I could find £10,000 of savings I would be a penny a litre better off. There's nowhere in my costs that I can save £10,000 in one big hit, but I might get there with a little bit here and there.

Then last week our milk price went down another penny, so the £10,000 disappeared before I'd saved it!

6 FEBRUARY 2016

I've been reading about an old theatre in Bristol that invented a thunder sound-effect by rolling wooden balls down a shuttering of planks and it was incredibly realistic. There is a connection. Lately we've been harvesting fodder beet. Fodder beet is normally harvested in November and occasionally in December. We all know what the weather has been like, no need for me to remind you. Inevitably the land is very wet and on rare frosty days it's very sticky. I've got a lot of fodder beet still in the ground, fodder beet that I hoped, and needed, to sell. Selling it is the difference between a cashflow that really struggles and a phone call from the bank manager! Not that it's hugely valuable, there's plenty of fodder beet about, so it's best not to be too clever about price, because it's got a shelf life and is perishable.

Sheep everywhere, those that are outside, have had a hard time in the wet, they've made a mess of root crops and grassland and it is farmers with sheep that are showing an interest in the beet. The other market place could be to digesters to turn beet into power. So what have beet to do with wooden balls rolling down a chute? Well, the beet harvester has a hopper on it that accumulates 3-4 tons of beet and then it stops and tips the hopperful into my trailer. As the first beet hit the metal floor of the trailer, they do so with a rumbling noise like theatrical sound-effect 'thunder'. In fact I would defy anyone to differentiate which is which. Strange the things you think of when you are sitting on a tractor.

★★★

When you are carting fodder beet, you take one hopperful off the harvester and you sit waiting for it to accumulate the next hopperful. Two of these hoppers make up a load on your trailer and away you go to tip it on the concrete, back at the buildings. There are two strips of beet left in the field and the harvester is working up and down the strips. I'm just sitting there on my tractor waiting and I see a group of pheasants making their way along the one strip. There are four cocks and about a dozen hens. They are totally unhurried in their progress towards me. I find this quite surprising as today has been a shooting day and pheasants get 'moved' about and disorientated. It's late afternoon, a time when a clean living pheasant is thinking of going to bed. And I look around me to see just where they are heading.

There is no obvious roosting place near me but soon they are all around me. I'm at the end of the field and they pop over the hedge into a grass field. They strut about a bit, do a bit of preening, get some soil off their feet and then they all take off and glide down the valley to a small group of trees at least half a mile away. It's all quite relaxed and gives me the impression that they knew exactly where they were going to roost all the time. Sometime during the day they have probably been shot at, they could have been shot at twice, but there's a sort of pragmatism to their demeanour: 'Shame about the three that got shot, but life goes on.'

12 FEBRUARY 2016

Because we farm land at different sites, most days finds me travelling with tractor and trailer on the roads. This week there have been chicken sheds to clear out and I've also been carting ordinary farm-yard manure from the cattle sheds. Both sorts of manure take the journey to our high fields where it will be ploughed in, come the spring, and where it will do untold good.

Anything to do with intensive poultry seems to be emotive, which I find very strange. 'They' reckon that over 2 million chicken are eaten in the UK every day. Chicken are popular because they are cheap, nutritious and good to eat. I've no idea how many eggs are eaten, it must be several dozen. Lots and lots of people find the production of chicken and eggs objectionable and yet lots and lots of people think eating them is OK! How do you balance that out?

Even poultry manure is stigmatised, yet it is the most

wonderful manure. If it is ploughed in on a regular basis, earthworm populations double and treble. A high earthworm population is an important yardstick that tells you that all is well with the world, or in this case, all is well with your soil. And because a chicken's digestive system needs grit to grind their food in the crop, and laying hens need calcium to make eggshells, when you put on poultry manure, you are putting calcium into the soil at the same time. You would have thought that the poultry story in this country was a good story but there is a minority that would like to stop it. If you ask them what they would give people to eat instead, they don't have an answer. The silent majority just keep on buying, quite happy that they can buy a chicken for the very low price it is.

Anyway, I was really on the road with tractor and trailer, before that digression (sometimes digression is another word for a whinge). Nearly every journey turns into an adventure. My most usual journey takes in half a mile of B-road and about a mile and a half of narrow lanes. Take the bit on the B-road first. At this time of year, I'm in no rush. I quite enjoy the job, it's warm and dry in the cab, the radio works, so I'm in a good mood and what I don't cart today, I'll cart tomorrow. There are no lay-bys on this section of road but there are two straight stretches where the visibility is good. As soon as I get two vehicles behind me I pull over as often as I can, so that they can overtake me. And nine times out of ten, what do they do? They just sit there. I usually give them a couple of minutes, and when there is no reaction, I drive on. So they end up being stuck behind me for long enough.

The narrow lane bit calls for a different set of driving skills. There's hardly a place where two cars can pass, let alone a car pass a tractor and trailer. The only opportunities to pass me are where there are gateways. I always have the beacons flashing on top of the cab so people can see me at a distance but invariably they ignore that and drive right up to me. So we sit there staring at each other. They have a gateway perhaps 20 yards behind them: they won't back up, but they expect me to back tractor and trailer 50 or 60 yards to the gateway behind me. Sometimes we end up facing each other at a gateway. I gesture, in friendly manner, for them to pull in to the gateway. Less friendly, they gesture for me to pull into the gateway. There is no way a 12 foot gateway will contain my tractor and trailer but there's plenty of room for a car!

The ones that really amuse me are the ones that get stuck behind me on the narrow lanes. I know that there is nowhere that I can let them by until we get to the B-road, so best to press on. In theory I could go just past a gateway, they could pull into the space, I could reverse and they could pull out in front. This is much how trains pass each other using a siding. This is a complicated manoeuvre and a sure recipe for disaster. It could end in a broken wing mirror and the kiss that a trailer could give a nice new car is to be avoided. So it's best to press on, a mile isn't far in the grand scheme of things.

So cars appear in my mirrors behind me. Firstly they put their lights on to make sure that I know they are there. Then, in my wing mirrors, I see that they have got a wheel on the grass, just to see if they can squeeze by. But there's not room so they try the same tactic on the other side as they try to pass me on the inside. My last load today and a car does all this, plus a bit of headlight flashing. There's 24 gears on this tractor and the digital display tells me that I'm apparently in D2 which is gear 22. There's a little stubby lever that changes gear electronically so I give it a couple of flicks and drop back to C6. Patience is a virtue and it's fortunate for the car driver that I am prepared to slow down a bit to teach them that. When we get to the B-road, the last 20 yards widens into room for two cars, so this car pulls alongside me at the white line although it is technically on the wrong side of the road. We both wait because there's two cars coming down the road. They both want to turn in to the lane but can't because this car is blocking their way. So he has to reverse back behind my trailer in order for them to exit the B-road. Me, I'm clear to go, and I do. And the 'naughty' car is going the same way, so once again he is stuck behind me. When I go in to the house for my tea, Ann asks what I've been doing all day, and I answer, 'Just carting muck'. But that's only the half of it.

20 FEBRUARY 2016

The shooting season has been and gone, thank goodness, in that life, and Saturday nights in particular, should return to some sort of normality. Whether 'the shooters' will be about on Saturday nights or if they are sent to a clinic to dry out, remains to be seen. Although the shooting season draws to a close every year on the same date, the actual shooters seem to drag it out as long as they can. I used to love shooting, but I don't remember being like that. Shooting should finish at the end of January, so how does that include the 1st February? Some shoots I know of went out on three occasions in the last six days of the season. It's always annoying to me, that the pheasants seem to know when it's finished. On 2nd February I came across three cocks on the lane, who all stood their ground. The day before they would have dived for cover as soon as they heard the truck approach.

I always devote space at this time of year to the harbingers of spring. But, however do you do that in a crazy year like this? I've lived here over 50 years and never before seen a daffodil in flower in January. We are quite high up where we live, about 650 feet, and you don't have to go very far to get to a lower level, six miles away, and spring flowers are out a month earlier than around here.

In the past I've struggled to find a daffodil for St David's day, 1st March. I've often said that the best I could find is a bud with just a bit of yellow visible and I've given it ten minutes in the microwave to bring it into flower. Some people have believed me!

A mile away from here, across the fields, are two large lakes. They reckon there are 70 to 80 swans on these lakes. Every day you can see pairs of swans searching the neighbourhood for a nesting site that affords more privacy. There's some low lying fields between us and the lakes and in the winter there are patches of water lying here and there. Every year you can see swans setting up home next to these small depressions. By the time their eggs hatch the water has long dried up. We've got a pond in our front field, it's about as big as a tennis court. Every day, pairs of swans check it out, but they never land. So what's wrong with it? Canada geese nest there every year. I don't mind Canada geese but I would rather some swans. My wife dreams of having swans. I've put 'rescue' swans there twice but they've never stayed long. They probably lie with all the others on those lakes.

My favourite armchair is opposite the window in our sitting room and through that I can see right across the valley. And 90% of the time there are a pair of red kites to be seen, as they tirelessly cover the valley looking for food. They must have found a good food source because they are back and forth over the same fields all day long. I suspect that the food is worms and grubs. It's the time of year when they have decided where to nest. I've looked for a suitable isolated tree for them and can't locate one but that doesn't mean that they can't. Their effortless high speed flight takes them in very short time to several woods. Their preferred option is a conifer, one with a spread to its branches that allows easy access for when they return home. A Scots pine is their ideal choice, it has an openness that allows them to come and go without damaging their flight feathers and they can usually find a place for the nest on a limb that is under the canopy of another, thus providing shelter for eggs and chicks.

5 MARCH 2016

If I go out at night, which I do, I can turn either left or right and within a mile I nearly always see a barn owl. One of nature's finest sights, one of nature's most beautiful birds. Two birds are hunting the verges at the side of the road. Not an ideal place to hunt, because their flight often takes them onto the road itself and they hunt at car height. You usually see them well in advance in your headlights, plenty of time to react. But I've several times seen a barn owl in the lights of a car in front of me, and that car has driven right through the owl. It seems deliberate and it makes me so angry.

★★★

New evidence has in recent months proved that the animal fats contained in dairy products are in fact good for you. This new evidence came after 30 to 40 years of advice to the contrary. Advice that was paid for by the people who made margarines and spreads! Now we are told that not only was that advice wrong, completely wrong, but that artificial spreads are not without their negatives, because they are high in damaging trans-fatty acids. And also cooking in vegetable-based oils gives off chemicals! So having said all that, why have the yellow tubs of spread continued to turn up on our kitchen table, just as they have for 30 or 40 years? Habit, that's why. They have continued to find their way into the supermarket trolley because they always have. So I passed a remark one day at breakfast that we should stop buying these spreads, that we should buy butter, that we support our own dairy industry. And lo and behold, a week later the last of the spread was gone and a butter dish took its place. Now, I would be the first to admit that butter takes more managing. It won't spread straight from the fridge. If it comes straight from the fridge you have to put it on your toast in thick slabs. So our butter dish started out on the worktop next to the fridge but now I see that it lives on the worktop near to the Rayburn. As I will explain later, I was very surprised that my 'move to butter' advice was heeded.

But this job is nowhere near finished. About ten years ago we had TB in our herd so while that was going on we thought it sensible to buy the milk for the house from a shop, pasteurised milk. Pasteurisation removes any danger of TB from milk. For 40 years we had used unpasteurised milk, straight from the tank, in our house. My two children were reared on unpasteurised milk with no apparent ill effects. Apart that is, that they now seem to go to the pub more often than even I do. Anyway, continuing on with the same theme as that I used with the butter, I noticed the milk that we are still buying is skimmed. No need for that, I tell the assembled family: all the best bits, the bits that contain nutrition, the minerals and the calcium, many of those are taken out in the process of removing some fat, much better to buy milk with it 'all' still in there. Better to buy whole milk I tell them. Whole milk is only 3.6% fat anyway, so we are hardly talking double cream, are we? And next time I go to make some tea, there it is, whole milk. So I've had my way with the butter and the milk. Surprise on surprise!

And why am I surprised? Because of cereals, that's why. I usually have a bowl of cereal at midday, in fact my preferred lunch is a bowl of cereal and a sleep in the chair. Twenty years ago a new sort of breakfast cereal turned up here. I won't name it, but it's got fibre and fruit in it, it's supposed to be healthier. And I made the mistake of saying how much I liked it. Why was it a mistake? Because we've had no other cereal through the door for twenty years. Other people seem to have a cereal mix. If you stay at my brother's, for example, they put four or five different cereals on the breakfast table. And they have a choice of yoghurts (one has honey in it!) but we have just the same cereal every time.

To be fair to our actual farmhouse kitchen table, it has more character than my brother's. Mine has a pile on it. The pile begins life with last week's magazines, newspapers and unopened post. It is given new life with the addition of more of the same plus all manner of stuff which includes grandson's clothes. This pile grows and grows until it either falls off or there is not room for us to sit down. Whatever, the back of it is removed by wheelbarrow and recycled with a match. The question I now have in my mind is this: if I managed to get butter and a change of milk, should I take a chance and try to get a change of cereal? I've been pondering this for two weeks now and have not yet reached a conclusion. I'm thinking at the moment to bank my two victories and leave it at that. Sometimes you should quit while you're ahead.

12 MARCH 2016

Now here's a strange thing. There's a crossroad on the lane I use every day, to get to our other land. It's a different sort of crossroad to the ones you get normally because it's a crossroad that gives you five options. That's probably why it's called 'The Five Turnings'. We are very imaginative around here. For more years that I care to remember a kestrel lived near this crossroad. It had perfected a technique whereby it popped out in front of you, especially if you were on a tractor. It would fly, at tractor bonnet height about five yards in front of you for half a mile. Small birds would come out of the hedge as they heard the noise of the approaching tractor. Often they would try to cross over to the other hedge. And the kestrel would catch them. There are rich pickings to be had when small birds are fledging. Then for three years the kestrel disappeared. But now there is a kestrel back, once again using the tractor to flush out a meal. If it's the same kestrel, where has it been? If it's a 'new' one, which I suspect it is, where did it learn this trick? From its mother?

★★★

I really love watching people. One of the best places is at those Sunday lunch carveries. We went to one last Sunday, to mark a family birthday. It's one of the best locally, they get over 100 people every Sunday. The body language on show is wonderful. Most people affect a sort of nonchalance as they arrive and find a seat, trying to hide their eager anticipation of the feast that is yet to come. Then the carvery opens and most people hang back, reluctant to be seen as the first to go. Others have no such inhibitions and are away as soon as they can. This is all the stimulus the second wave needs.

They don't want to be seen to be too eager (greedy), so they affect the laid-back walk, it's as if they are out for a stroll, not bothered if they get there. But they know exactly where they are going. They are going towards the delicious smells of that food and all their instincts tell them to break into a trot. If you think I've made all this up, have a look yourself next time you go out for Sunday lunch.

But all this is nothing in comparison with the triumphant 'return' journey. The plate of food is carried carefully before them at chest height. Eyes are darting right and left, to make sure everyone can see. 'Look what I've got' – no king from the East bore gifts more proudly. And only Egyptian pharoahs built greater pyramids. The pile of food defies gravity. I've always thought that buffet means wastage and so it proves. When you go to one of those rare functions where drinks are free, people abandon half-consumed drinks and go for a fresh one. Lifelong beer drinkers move to spirits. I reckon that when the staff start to move in to collect used plates, 20-30% of food is carried back again. Not that this bothers the 'wasters' because they are moving in on the puddings. I ask a staff member what happens to all the food that is wasted. 'It goes in the bin.' So in a corner of my mind I'm telling myself that I wish I owned a business like this that turned over so much money in just a few hours. And my mind adds that if I did own this business, there would be a couple of pig-sties out at the back where I could feed all that food waste. I know that you are not allowed to feed food waste to pigs but doing things you are not supposed to has never been a big issue for me. The waitress is back and she tells me that all the kitchen food that is not used goes in the bin as well, so I make a mental note to build three pig-sties not two. To see so much money changing hands so quickly is another reminder that I have spent my life at the wrong end of the food chain. And if there are other people watchers present, do they see me displaying the same sort of eager mannerisms? I send someone to fetch mine. Very good it was too: I ate it all. Except the Yorkshire pudding.

19 MARCH 2016

We need a new bull. We've sold our old bull and we need a 'new' young one. The breed of bull we want is a Limousin. It's a French breed (bet you'd guessed that); it will breed useful beef-cross calves when mated with our cows and it will be quiet enough, from a public safety point of view, to turn out in the fields with our heifers. And just to round off its suitability as a breed, it is an easy calving breed so it's fine to use with those heifers.

We will buy this young bull at the same place we bought his predecessor. I've a friend who runs a herd of about 120 beef suckler cows. Amongst that herd he has a few pedigree Limousin cows. These cows are mated with a pedigree Limousin bull. So to all intents they are pedigree offspring. They are not registered, they don't have any 'papers', but then neither do I.

So how it works is this. I go down to where he has a pen of 12-month-old bulls that he is fattening and within that group are half a dozen of these pure bred Limousins, and of these there are three real beauties that are just what we need. We will make a final decision in a month's time, because he needs one more clear TB test before he can sell anything.

TB casts its cloud over everything you do with cattle. I went down yesterday to have a look at them, and very good they looked too. It's one of the pleasures of farming: you buy a new bull, you use your best judgement, and at a future date, when his calves are on the ground, you see if your judgement is any good.

I prefer buying bulls to the days when I used to buy tups (rams.) A pedigree tup that is presented clipped at the autumn sales is really a sculpture in wool and you don't get a real look at what you have bought until you let him go after you've taken the wool off him at shearing time.

Buying a new bull is a marker of the passage of your time as a farmer. You are always planning for the future and in this case for the calves you may have in 12 months' time. But farming is such a long-term project, that most of what you plan is on a longer timescale. For example you put a cow to a dairy bull today, hoping to breed a dairy heifer that will start milking in three years' time and you hope that you will still be milking her in ten years.

But this year has a very different feel to it. We are going through the motions of a long-term vision. Just as we always have. But there is a very real chance that we won't be dairy farming in 12 months' time. This year's budget shows a loss so we have to borrow money to cover that loss. On 1st April our milk price goes down a further 1.3p which is about £1000 a month to us. We haven't put that reduction in the budget yet. There's no way we intend to carry on like that. What's the point? Too much milk they say, but we are producing the same amount that we produced three years ago. I know that we haven't contributed to the surplus but we have, for some reason, to share the pain. I am looking ahead buying this bull, yet at the same time, at the back of my mind, the possibility that in 12 months' time I won't be a milk producer any more and it has a strange feel about it. It isn't a comfortable feeling.

★★★

I know a man who lives in an isolated cottage in a clearing in a wood. It sounds idyllic and, come the spring and summer, it is. But there's snow on the tops around here today, and that's where his cottage is, high up in a wood. It's a very small cottage. It started life as one room down and one up. By the standards of today it is very, very basic. There's a tin shed, cum-lean-to, at the back that houses his diesel generator so he has electricity, of a sort. His toilet came indoors about twenty years ago into a corner of his downstairs room and this created what he calls his 'bathroom'. This 'bathroom' is very small, it contains neither bath nor shower, and should you so wish, you could sit on the toilet and use the washbasin at the same time. What's that? How does he bathe? I've no idea, but he's always very clean and tidy. Two years ago, he bought one of these very efficient wood burning stoves. There is a problem with it. His house is very small and the stove he chose is top of the range, a very large one. One that is designed to heat quite a large house. He was telling me about it the other day. 'It's a really good stove, in fact it's too good, the house isn't just warm, it's too hot. I have to keep the door open 24 hours a day to make it bearable. Trouble is, the door being open attracts a lot of vermin in.' He's a very polite man, and when he uses the word, vermin, you can safely assume that we are talking rats. But that's not the half of it. 'A squirrel came in last week and it was under my bed for two days before I could catch it.'

26 March 2016

Lambing has started, most of my friends are at it now, but there's not the usual excited buzz about its arrival. Most sheep farmers tell me that their returns from last year's lambs are down £20-25 a lamb on the previous year, so they've had a good kicking on price this year. I don't follow it very closely but a lot of lamb is exported so exchange rates haven't helped and there's always the worry that, if the lambs go to Spain or Greece, the money might not turn up. Centre stage on the banter front is the friend who lambs his ewes a mile from where he lives, so he and his son take it in turns to sleep there in a caravan. It's a lot easier to turn out in the early hours if you are already fully dressed than if you are nice and cosy in a warm bed. When I used to keep sheep I would stay fully dressed all night and snatch some sleep in the sitting room. This would last for about a month, yes, sometimes with the same clothes on, and after that month I would be going around the same shape as a settee. We are teasing the man who sleeps in the caravan, that if a ewe is close to lambing, he gets her into the caravan with him, so he can keep an eye on her without getting out of bed.

★★★

I know of a young couple who keep sheep in some fields over the road from where they live. He's at work all day and she is with those ewes all day long, to keep an eye on them. I took them a load of fodder beet the other day and she was telling me this. She had a ewe that was making a start on lambing one afternoon but she also had to walk about 200 yards to meet her young children off the school bus. The ewe was just starting to lamb and she didn't really want to leave her, but in this day and age, you don't leave small children unaccompanied either. So she goes to collect the children and how long was she away, ten or fifteen minutes? By the time she had got back the ewe had given birth to one lamb, and was lying down trying to give birth to a second. The first-born lamb of two, has a tough start in life. It's born, its mother gets to her feet, makes a fuss of it, then she has to leave it while she gets back down to give birth to the second. But they don't all have as tough a start as this particular lamb. Because by the time the mother had got back to the field there were three ravens attending to it. They had pecked out its eyes, they had eaten its tongue and had started to peck out its back passage. There's a river bordering this particular field and we could see three ravens sitting in the tops of some alder trees. 'We can't do anything about them because they are protected and there are bird watchers looking at the ravens all the time.'

Unpleasant as it might be, it's important that we consider the probable scene a bit further. Within minutes the newly-born lamb would be on its feet, prompted by the ministrations of its mother. The mother would then have to lie down again, to get on producing the other lamb, and the first born would just stand there, soaking wet, completely at a loss about the world it now found itself in. And the ravens would move in to do their worst. You can rear a lamb with no eyes, it will cope quite well in a flock situation, but a lamb without a tongue just can't suck. How on earth did the mother describe the scene to her young children?

There are hundreds of ravens around here. They are glorified by wildlife groups who put their numbers into the hundreds. They don't want to know anything about the damage they do and the suffering they cause. I've got nothing against ravens, but why do we have to have so many? If I had lambs, and ravens were attacking them, it wouldn't be a problem. My eyesight is not that good, and over the sights of a 12 bore shotgun, a raven, which is protected, looks very much like a carrion crow, which isn't.

★★★

There is a regular roadside traffic 'purge' around here, by the police and trading standards. A friend of mine was stopped recently and whilst they were checking his truck, he was breathalysed. They found he contained too much red wine. They also found that his truck contained too much red diesel. It just wasn't his day was it?

★★★

We were driving through a local village (well it's nearly big enough to be a town) early on Sunday evening and there were about 100 people standing on the side of the road. An adjoining road had been cordoned off by police cars. At the pub later on, the incident was the main topic of conversation. The latest news was that there was a gunman roaming about. That two armed police response teams were present and also a squad of riot police. Apparently the incident was so serious that anyone that found themselves in the fish and chip shop had to stay there and an armed policeman had to guard the door. There's worse places to be locked in! It doesn't get much more serious than that, does it? It's Monday morning before we get to the truth of it all. It seems that a local man had been off for the day shooting pigeons with some friends. On his return, his friends had dropped him off on the main road, and he had strolled the 50 yards to his home with his shotgun under his arm.

2 April 2016

Now here's a strange story. As most of you know, I want another corgi. But I don't want one badly enough that I am prepared to pay the sort of money that has an eight next to the £ sign. Just to put that into the perspective of the world I live in, I need to sell five litres of milk to get a £1, so that's 4,000 litres plus for a corgi pup! But my grandchildren quite like the idea of a new puppy about the place so they are always checking the internet and to be fair, they often find cheaper ones. But they are only cheaper because they are corgi crossed, probably inadvertently, with something else. Who wants to pay £400 for a corgi-cross spaniel? Certainly not me.

Last Saturday my grandson's girlfriend says she has found a litter of corgi pups that were £400. That's still a lot of money but I've got a birthday this week and I was starting to think that if we all chipped in we might get £400 together. I was also starting to think, as a confirmed sceptic or cynic (I was brought up to think that you should never believe anything you hear and only half of what you see), that if corgi pups were making £800 to £850, why would you want to sell one for £400? So we get up the pictures of the pups and they are lovely, and they have papers, injections and have been wormed, are only to go to good homes and are quite handy in the next county. I remember thinking, all this sounds too good to be true.

So we start up this email dialogue and I keep getting these very long replies. The more the emails went on, the more suspicious I became. So we get to the position where these pups will only be sold to people who commit to sending a monthly report and a photo to confirm satisfactory progress, oh and by the way, the pups are not in the next county, they are in the Isle of Man and they belong to a recently deceased relative and the advertisers just want them to go to good homes. There's now a strong smell of rat to all this. Have you ever been to the Isle of Man? I have. And I've driven around the TT course. But not on a motorbike, in a Ford Fiesta. Anyway, it's not the handiest of places to get to. Time to call their bluff. But whilst I am giving that some thought, yet another email arrives. It says that the family have given the matter a lot of thought and decided to let us have a puppy, that it would arrive by pet courier (didn't know there were such things), that I should send the £400 plus £100 for the courier and the puppy would arrive on Monday afternoon. So here we go, 'Thank you very much for letting us have a puppy but we always like to see the pup with its mother and will be over on the Isle of Man on Monday morning to collect it.' Surprise, surprise, we didn't hear another word. Did the puppy ever exist? I doubt it. If it did, it might have started life in Eastern Europe, but I just think it was all a £500 scam. It's probably nothing at all to do with the Isle of Man. I've spent most of my life up to my knees in what comes from under a cow's tail, which serves me well, as I'm quite good at spotting faeces of all kinds.

★★★

We are driving back from Cardiff after the last rugby international and we are talking about lambing. There's a vet in the car and two people (I'm one), who used to keep sheep but don't anymore. So the one companion is telling of the time that he was trying to get his ewes into the lambing shed, but they wouldn't go. His temper was getting very frayed and he was starting to fall out with his dog. There was only the dog and him there, so to be fair who else was he to blame?

Things got worse and worse and eventually the inevitable happened and the dog slunk off to sulk somewhere, giving hurt looks over its shoulder as it went. No matter how he tried to beg or cajole the dog in a very different tone of voice, it had had enough and the sulk was likely to last two or three hours.

He's still got to get the sheep into the shed so he goes to get his wife to help. This is always a big mistake, because you are substituting a wife for a dog and all you get is a re-run of the previous fall-out that you had with the dog, only it happens quicker, because the wife, unlike the dog, will answer back. So the inevitable happens, the sheep are still not in the shed and very sharp words have been exchanged.

They have come to the end of this particular road and both set off home, the sheep are still in the field and the falling out has been serious enough that they take different routes back home so as to avoid speaking to each other. So my friend is trudging back along a hedgerow and he gives vent to his frustrations, out loud. I won't go into too much detail but blankety blank women and blankety blank dog were mentioned several times. So preoccupied was he with his ranting that he did not realise that his wife was the other side of the hedge listening, 'I heard all that, I shall never help you with the sheep again.' And nor did she.

I only made the wife/dog mistake once. My wife is a very accomplished lamber. She could sort out the odd badly presented lambs better than I could. Late one night I fetched her out to deliver some triplets, there were heads and legs everywhere but she sorted them out. When we were back in the kitchen cleaning our arms and hands up, she discovered she had lost her wedding ring. So we went back up to the lambing shed, caught the ewe, she put her hand back in and there it was.

9 April 2016

After the shooting season finishes, the keeper usually disappears for a couple of months. I always assumed that the first month was to catch his breath after six months of seven days a week, either rearing pheasants, or organising the shoots, and making sure everything went well. Then I knew he had a busy month doing the lambing at the farm where he works full-time. Then, and only then, would he want a catch-up.

This year the catch-up meeting was a month earlier than usual. So I ask him why, has he finished lambing already? He tells me that his boss has sold all the sheep. They weren't making any money, so what's the point of all that work? It's a question lots of farmers are asking themselves, and goodness knows where it will all end. What he wants to know, in the catch-up, is what crops we will have in each field. We grow a lot more root crops now, root crops have taken the place of the maize we used to grow. Maize is an expensive crop to grow and the height above sea level where we live, makes it a bit marginal. It always looked a big crop when you looked at it over a gate, but the feed value of maize is always in the cobs and the starch they provide, and the feed value of the last crop we had grown had been disappointing.

So the root crops we now grow are of great interest to the keeper because pheasants love spending their day in root crops and a patch of roots, in the right place, can enhance a day's shooting no end. He's looking for a bit of tweaking to how we harvest the roots, tweaking that will help the shoot. The conversation goes a bit like this. 'When you get that fodder beet up, you couldn't just leave an acre in that corner until the end of January for the pheasants?'

And if you do, he puts feeders out there, and he puts straw along the hedgerow for them to scratch about in, and come shooting day, the pheasants are flushed out of this sanctuary and instinctively fly back to their rearing pen, and the guns are waiting in strategic places along a very predictable flight path.

'Just' is a very big word round here, its meaning knows no bounds with my farming neighbours. 'You couldn't *just* let me put some ewes and lambs on that nice bit of grass you've got down by the wood?' 'You couldn't *just* let me fill my Land Rover with a few fodder beet for some ewes I've got with triplets?' So you say yes, of course you can, and you go past the fodder beet clamp and the Land Rover has now got a trailer behind it!

I always try to help the keeper with his 'tweaking'. There's a bit of partnership involved that sees us helping each other. His keeping gets him around my fields at night and very early mornings and he sees our stock at times when we are not about ourselves. I get texts from him that might say 'Cow calved up the hollow, both OK.' It's the 'both OK' bit that's most important, because it tells you that you do not need to go to see them with any urgency.

Anyway, we agree on some 'tweaking' and he is well pleased, so I introduce a 'just' request of my own.

We had a flock of about 12 lapwings that bred on some root ground last year. I had worried about how the chicks would survive with so many winged predators in the area, something I could do very little about, but I also worried what the chicks would do for water as they were born on a high dry field about half a mile from any watercourse. So here we go, me to the keeper: 'If those lapwings nest again this year, you couldn't just help me to look after them?' As I expect, his response is excellent. He just loves to do anything that helps wildlife. Which is a far cry from the stereotype image most people have of gamekeepers.

I have some small areas of roots to put in later on in the year. It's a part of what's called 'greening', I have to put 5% of my arable and temporary grass in to other crops. This year we will use this as an opportunity to help the lapwings. We will grow varieties of roots that will encourage insects for the chicks to feed on. There will be roots with larger leaves that will provide shade from the sun and cover from predators. That still leaves the issue of water. What we will do, because we will know where the nests are, is put some poultry drinkers out in strategic places. I know where I can nick some of those. There's plenty in our chicken sheds, they won't miss half a dozen. They don't need to be very big: how much water does a lapwing chick that's as big as your thumbnail actually drink?

The keeper's enthusiasm for this project knows no bounds. 'I'll build some scrapes' he says. Whenever people are talking about helping lapwings they talk of 'scrapes': I'm not really sure what they are, but I'm not admitting it. If I keep quiet, I expect I'll find out in the fullness of time. I think it's an area of bare soil, but what its role is, I don't know. And so we go our separate ways. He's happy, I'm fairly happy, though I rarely admit it, and in due course I hope there'll be some happy lapwings. What does it say in the song? 'Spread a little happiness as you go by.'

16 APRIL 2016

There are several milestones that mark the passage of the year. I always think that when the winter barley goes into ear, the rest of the year goes by quite quickly, in fact, I have been known to say that once the winter barley is in ear, before you know where you are, it's Christmas. Lambing, shearing, sowing maize and the various harvests you undergo, they all mark the passage of the year. There's a local contractor who does a lot of silage work and we put a tractor and rake into the gang. Mid-March and we were put on standby: the contractor had a client who had a field he wanted to plough but there was a lot of grass on it. So he decided to make it into silage. Silage in March! It completely threw my seasonal calendar out. Whatever next? Would the nights start drawing in, before they had started drawing out? As it happened, the March silage wasn't done, and order was restored.

★★★

The cock pheasants are scattered about the hedgerows at regular intervals, like the sentinels that they are, keeping guard over the hen or hens that they have thus far accumulated into a harem. Those hens are secreted away in the adjacent hedge where they are laying their eggs. They come out once or twice a day to feed and the cock pheasants avail themselves of their conjugal rights, very forcibly. Unfortunately some of these hedgerows are on the side of the lanes and roads and that is where the cock pheasants often maintain their vigil, sometimes with unfortunate consequences.

There's been one such cock standing in a lane that I use several times a day. We're quite busy on field work and each time I went past I would have to slow right down for him to move to one side. Cock pheasants are very aggressive at this time of year and his body language was very clear: 'This is my road, but I can see that you are very busy, so I'm going to let you past.' And he would step gracefully aside. He had been doing that for about a week. He had been within about ten yards of the same place all of that time. It's a one car lane, you have to pull on the grass verge to pass another vehicle. But it was on a very straight piece of the lane and you could easily see the cock pheasant from a 100 yards in either direction.

Yesterday I went to see my heifers and I had to pass the cock pheasant. We went through the usual courtesies and I went past him. Ten minutes later, when I returned, he was dead, his mangled carcase all over the road. So mangled was he, he was clearly hit by a vehicle travelling at speed. A few days ago I was following a car on a road a few miles away and there was a covey of about 12 partridge on the road. The car in front drove straight through them, there wasn't even a flicker of his brake lights. Most of them were left dead or dying on the road. There must be some very important people about, whose lives are so busy they don't even have the time to ease off the accelerator for other creatures.

23 APRIL 2016

This week has seen tractors in most of our fields, putting fertiliser on growing crops or putting chicken manure on our grassland. Despite having a dryish spring there are still plenty of wet places in some fields, a legacy, I am sure, of the very wet December. We usually do these jobs a lot earlier, and I've been getting a bit twitchy about the timing, but as far as ground conditions go, we are early enough. But it's a late spring. The grass is not growing much yet, not good for the cows, but it's good for the fodder beet sales, especially to sheep farmers, and as we still have a lot left, that's OK.

On the wildlife front we are very disappointed that in the last three weeks we have not seen one lapwing. But the spring is late so there is still time for them to come and nest, fingers crossed. Their nests don't take much building, just the depression made with a cow's foot seems to suffice. This was going to be our year to help the lapwings raise their chicks successfully and if they don't turn up, that's going to be difficult.

I was discussing lapwings with someone I know who is a member of a wildlife group. The area where his group is based had tried to do a lapwing census and a part of that census had revealed that they had vast areas where they couldn't find evidence of one chick being reared. 'I've only just joined a wildlife group,' he tells me, 'and already it is obvious to me that there are too many predators about.' Now that statement has a familiar ring to it. I wonder where I've heard that before? He goes on to tell me that he has a relative in a wildlife group many miles away and last year they found nine lapwing nests and put posts in the ground nearby and put cameras on the posts. Seven of the nests were destroyed by badgers. At the remaining two that hatched out, there was no sign of any chicks after 12 hours. He tells me that this group had been sworn to secrecy about the role of badgers. 'They didn't want any anti-badger messages getting out there, it's a very sensitive time for badgers!' Tell me about it! If you want to have a balance in nature then you have to make choices.

★★★

This week is dog microchip week. I'm all in favour of that, but I haven't had my dog Mert, micro-chipped. He's not big into technology, he's never asked for a mobile phone. He's old, doesn't go far. If truth be told, he's getting old and grumpy, a bit like me. If you tried to lift him into the truck to take him to the vets, you would probably get bitten, as would any vet who tried to micro-chip him. And, for that matter, anyone who subsequently tried to read the micro-chip. No, probably best to leave well alone.

★★★

We've been quite busy lately on all sorts of jobs. Next on our list is to sow the spring barley. Seems a bit late but it's about right for around here. Stephen is having three days off next week so I tell him I will get the ground ploughed while he's away. I know he's not keen on me using his tractor and plough so I know he will have

30

it all ploughed before he goes away. Not as dull as I look, me, which is fortunate. He goes up one late afternoon to start ploughing and, hurray! the lapwings are back. Well, ten of them. We'll have the barley sown before they nest.

30 April 2016

I've been on an adventure. A friend of mine is off buying a dog and he asks me if I want to come for a ride. Our journey is to take us to a city in the Midlands and the time of day is what traffic bulletins call the rush hour, but what we call around here knocking-off time. Where we live is very, very quiet from a traffic point of view so this is a bit of a new experience. As we approach our first big island, he asks me if he's in the right lane. As if I'm likely to know! When I drive around a big roundabout, I look in the rear-view mirror and my grandchildren are closing their eyes. I advise him to move one lane out and we emerge out of the roundabout in the correct lane, unscathed, so after that he defers to me as some sort of expert. The journey, in busy conditions, proves a theory I have: if you have an oldish vehicle that is filthy and carries the odd scratch, other road users give you a wide berth, because they assume that you are not too bothered about any coming together that might occur. The truck we are travelling in is admirable for this purpose. I think my friend has had it about six years and he's washed it once. The interior has been cleaned out never. I have brought my satnav with us and as we get nearer to our destination, I try to fire it up, but there's too much dirt in the cigarette lighter socket and I can't get the connection in. Anyway we eventually get to our destination.

What we are here to buy is a spaniel. I knew a man once who called them 'spanles', a pronunciation I loved and which I persist in using. But we are not here to buy any old spaniel, we are here to buy a Clumber spaniel. Clumbers are very rare and a working strain of Clumber is rarer still. Working strain is defined by going out shooting. It's a well-built stocky sort of breed, a stalwart, a sort of superhero of the spaniel world. They are of a working strain, the mother and father are there with the pups; the grandmother, we are told, has royal connections! We knew exactly what sort of dog we were there to buy because they also had a dog there from a previous litter of the same mating. It was a bit like the canine equivalent of 'here's one I prepared earlier'.

My friend says he will have one (of course he will, he's been looking for one for a long time), and selects a little bitch. He puts it in the back of his truck with his Springer spaniel bitch that has also come for the ride and off we go home. We hear a couple of whimpers from the pup and one low key growl from the Springer. When we get home they are both asleep, cwtched up together.

When I was first married I had a black Labrador bitch that I used to breed pups from. On two separate occasions the vet appeared on my yard with beautiful Labrador bitches in the back of his car. He told me that they had been taken to his surgery to be put down as their owners no longer wanted them. He didn't want to euthanise young healthy dogs and had thought of me. In due course a Labrador dog turned up in the same circumstances so I suppose we became what some people would call a puppy farm, but it wasn't like that at all.

I didn't breed pups for long because these Labs would have such large litters. If you had a litter of ten pups, which wasn't uncommon, you could probably sell six quite easily. The ones that were left would soon grow very quickly so that if someone turned up to buy one and they had small children with them, the pups would be so strong and boisterous they would knock the children down. Which wasn't a good sales point. Better not to breed them in the first place, which is what happened. It always used to amuse me that often when a family with young children turned up, mother and children would be making a fuss of these adorable black or yellow puppies and the father would be standing a little aloof and he might say, 'We haven't decided to have one yet.' And I would look at his family and the pups together and I would think, 'It's more than your life's worth to go away without one.' And the Labradors lived long and happy lives, which is more than they would have done if the vet had carried out his instructions.

★★★

As the land dries out and the season advances, spring work in the fields is the order of the day. Tractors are busy in the fields and the tractor days are getting longer. We get a report in the pub from one tractor driver that he was off to sow some spring barley. He had some spare bits and pieces for the drill in a shed, in a cardboard box. He put the box onto the floor of the cab and four mice jumped out. He managed to catch three but the fourth escaped under the seat. Seats on modern tractors are very sophisticated pieces of kit, with all sorts of adjustments for suspension, posture and comfort. There was no way that he could catch this last mouse. There's no easy way to say this, so I'll just say it. The mouse was killed, probably by the movement of the seat as it went up and down. And how does he know it's dead? Because the stench from its decomposing body is so bad he has to use an air freshener before he can get in the cab.

7 May 2016

It's a few weeks ago now, but Ann's daily paper ran a full page story about the huge fall in hedgehog numbers. I think the article was timed to coincide with a sort of National Hedgehog week. The writer placed the blame for this decline squarely on farmers. How do I react to this? Well it could be with indignation, but not too much. It's not too much because farmers are well used to getting the blame for all sorts of things. There's only 2% of the population who have a connection with farming, it's the sort of percentage that makes us an ethnic minority; folk like politicians and anyone else with an agenda can have a 'go' with a fair chance of a 'free' shot. So I thought about it, and I decided to think about it a bit longer and see if I do anything that would be a negative for your hedgehog.

The author of the article quoted the miles of hedgerows that had been removed since WWII but that's very naughty, because there's miles and miles of hedgerows been replanted since then. On this farm alone we've replanted about three miles of hedgerow that was removed by a previous occupier. Those who produce hedgerow plants and trees have been something of a growth industry in recent years so that particular jibe is unfair. But instead of leaping to the defence of farmers and farming, I've decided to think about it. What do I do that is to the detriment of hedgehogs? And then, eventually, I thought of slugs. Not the most endearing of creatures, your slug. But hedgehogs eat them. The slug for their part will decimate your crops. Sometimes they will take large areas, sometimes they will take the lot. Ask any keen gardeners what they think about slugs. But you can buy slug pellets that you spread on the land and this will, if you get the timing right, kill them. I don't do this as routine, I try to ascertain how many slugs are actually there. This can be done by putting, for example, a couple of empty fertiliser bags out on the ground, weighted down with some stones. Next day any adjacent slugs will be under the plastic and you can make a judgement on numbers. Slugs can take any crop that you sow, from grasses, brassicas, cereals, fodder crops, the lot.

At the back of your mind is always the need to grow enough food for your animals for next winter. So what would you do? Well only about 25% of your land is ploughed and cropped every year, the rest is down to grass. You don't need to put slug pellets onto established grassland and I only put them on crops that are at risk, and that doesn't really equate to the percentage decline in hedgehog numbers. So there must be other factors. One thing I take much more seriously than the killing of slugs, is killing insects. I avoid doing that at all costs.

But for two years on the trot I have tried to grow a crop of kale for winter feed on a nine acre field. And for two years that crop has failed because of flea beetles. They will completely remove a crop in a day or so, certainly before you can get the contractor there to spray them. We are going to try to grow kale on the same field again this year, not one to be beaten, me. This year we are going to try a different strategy. We will sow the same amount of kale seed per acre but on top of that we will all also grow other varieties such as fodder radish and mustard. This is the theory. Kale, after it germinates, goes to the two-leaf stage. This is the stage at which it is very vulnerable to things like slugs and flea beetle. We have slug pellets for the slugs but the flea beetle is the bigger problem. The two failed crops are testimony to this. But the flea beetle had shown that it had a preference for mustard and radish over kale. The theory is that whilst it is eating the mustard and radish, the kale will grow past the two-leaf stage and will be made of sterner stuff. Well that's the theory anyway.

Just to return to the hedgehog issue briefly. There are those of us in this minority that think that if you were to draw a graph that showed the decline of hedgehog numbers over the years and then you were to draw a graph that showed the increase in the number of badgers since they became protected, one line on that graph would be the exact opposite of the other. And that the growth of one species is connected to the decline of the other. It might be the view of a minority, but just because we are minority, doesn't mean that we are wrong. I was discussing the hedgehog issue with my son. He says that he's seen more hedgehogs this year than he's seen for a long time. Which is also true of me. OK so he's seen five and I've seen three, hardly a plague, but already it's more than we saw last year.

14 MAY 2016

We've got two pieces of spring barley, sown for over a week now, and nicely rolled in, even if I do say it myself. The one area is where we had fodder beet last year and on the very same piece of land there were eight lapwing nests. The last time we went over that land with some fertiliser, four of the nests had hatched out and you could easily see each cluster of chicks. We were hoping all of them would return this year but there was no sign of them. Then after we had finished our rolling, just two pairs turned up and they are showing all the signs of nesting. Our tactics at this stage are to keep well away, so I watch them from the truck at a good distance.

What does concern me is the number of carrion crows that are on the same ground. There's something about their strutting self-important gait that reminds me of the Fat Controller of Thomas the Tank Engine. What chance the lapwings have of successfully rearing chicks with all those carrion crows about, goodness only knows. I've tried to live my life without worrying about things that I can do nothing about. The carrion crows easily qualify for that category, so I try not to think about them too much. It's not easy.

★★★

This spring I've been absorbed in the farming jobs that just have to be done. We've had spring barley, fodder beet and grass seeds to put in. There's kale to put in as well, fertiliser to put on, and all this has to be done as well as you can do it, and in a timely fashion, before the first cut silage. You get absorbed by all this because it's proper farming and that's how it's always been, and if you did all this as well as you could, most years would be OK. But there's a real world beyond the farm gate and it's quite easy to forget about it. Yesterday's post brought us back to reality with a jolt. Another 0.5p a litre off our milk price on 1st June. That's 3.7 pence price drop this year alone. We sell about one million litres a year so every penny off costs me £10,000. We've sold this sort of amount for years so I don't feel responsible for any world surplus. And anyway the UK is not self-sufficient in dairy products, so the rest of the world is visiting its problems on UK dairy farmers. We can't go on like this. If you look up the word unsustainable in your dictionary it will probably say: milk prices.

★★★

I've never been good at small talk. I love talking to people but I always find it hard to start the conversation off with some low key sort of comment. What's the point of saying 'It's raining today' or 'Isn't it a nice day?' The person you are talking to can see that for themselves, they don't need you to tell them, do they? So I usually rely on someone else to start it all off, and even then I'm likely to give them a sarcastic reply. Like if they say it's raining today I'm very likely to say that I hadn't realised that. Anyway, we are just getting to the time of year when one popular opening gambit has run its course. To most farmers around here, you have been able to say, 'Finished lambing yet?' to which they invariably reply, 'Not quite, we've still got a few hogs left.' Hogs are one-year-old sheep that are having their first lambs and are usually lambed after the main flock.

We were out with some friends the other night and I asked him the lambing question, to which he gave me the usual reply. 'Tell Roger what happened last night,' his wife says. He won't tell me but she does. They'd been out for the evening and he says he will just pop to the lambing shed before they go to bed, as 'they've still got a few hogs left.' There's one of these hogs that's been looking like lambing and they've put it in a pen of hurdles on its own. He gets into the pen and decides to give it an internal examination. It's got two dead lambs inside it, and the lambs are starting to deteriorate. I leave that to your imagination. It occurs to me at this juncture that I talk quite a lot about death. Unfortunately, death is a fact of life! Where you get life then you also get death, and you get it in exactly the same proportion. That's just the way it is.

Anyway, he removes these two dead lambs and gives the sheep a shot of antibiotic to make her more comfortable. It wasn't fully explained to me how he got into the pen, but, whatever, he couldn't get out. He couldn't climb out because he has a bad leg and he couldn't pull himself out because he has a bad shoulder. So he contrived a sort of straddle of the top bar of the sheep hurdle, I suppose it was a bit like how high jumpers go over the bar (only in his case the bar would have come tumbling down.) But he didn't have a sort of air bag to land on, he fell on his back onto the concrete. He was already in a fair mess from removing the dead lambs but the concrete was covered with all the drainage liquid from the lambing pens. And he rolled over in all this 'mess'. His clothes were now so wet and filthy that he had no alternative but to remove them. His wife meanwhile is starting to wonder why he is so long, so she goes to the back door and switches the yard light on. The light catches him tiptoeing across the yard, totally naked, carrying a farming magazine he's found that he is using to hide his bits and pieces. 'You should have seen him!' she said. I wish I had.

21 MAY 2016

Although we've been busy about the fields, I've always got an eye open for the hares. And I see hares every day, but not in the numbers that I used to see them a couple of years ago. There's probably two reasons for this and the first has got to be the activities of hare coursers. Just how many have they slaughtered in two years? Only they will know that and they are not for telling. The other reason is a sort of side product to that. The hares that remain are much more nervous. And with good reason. I probably don't see them because they are off as soon as they hear me coming. In the past I used to know of several places where hares would 'lie up' for the day, and I could park just a few yards away and they wouldn't move. But if you want to know numbers you ask the keeper. 'You've got 20-30 hares up there.' How he counts them, goodness only knows but it's the best guide I have. I know of lots of farmers who would love to have 20–30 hares on their land. Some have asked me to take them to see the hares which I do. The sad thing is that two or three years ago the keeper was saying 'you've got 80-100 hares up there.'

★★★

Our family has been without a corgi for a couple for years now. And we miss it. I could fairly easily buy one, but they are £800 plus and we just don't have that sort of money. There's another member of our family, my youngest granddaughter, who also wanted a dog of her own. She wanted a pony as well, which caused a bit of family panic (not big on horses here), so a sheepdog puppy was quickly found for her. It wasn't fair really. Although a very young sheep-dog puppy served its purpose to begin with, as a pet for a little girl, it soon grew up and it soon discovered that there was a farmyard 100 yards away. So it soon escaped from its world of pink collars and fitted into a life for which it was intended, fetching cows and herding chickens and suchlike. To be fair it did return home at the end of its working day but it was so plastered with mud and cow muck it wasn't very welcome. So now it lives up at the farm most if its time and sleeps on an old settee in the outhouse where our central heating boiler is. She sleeps on the settee with my old dog Mert, whose duties she has largely taken over.

It's always been at the back of my mind that this sheepdog was not a realistic pet for a little girl and I remember telling the story to a neighbour 12 months ago. She has family connections to a vet and, vets often became aware of unwanted pets. I asked if they could keep their eye out for a nice little dog and last week they got in contact. They were aware of a Bichon Frise dog, only 18 months old. It was a cross, there seems to be some doubt about the one half of the cross, it is either a spaniel or a Lasso Apso (which is another breed I'm not sure how you spell). Ann and I went to fetch it. It's a lovely little dog. It lived on quite an upmarket housing estate, it was all open plan, so although I'm sure the dog went out a lot, I'm also sure it never went out off the lead. We were told how much it had cost and as it was free to us it must have depreciated at £2 a day. We got it back home and delivered it to my granddaughter. She was a bit cautious because it just wouldn't stop barking. (It wasn't just a bark, it was a yelping sort of bark.) It didn't stop yelping/ barking for three days. You've just got to be patient in a situation like this. This was dog-speak that said, 'I've been taken away from my family and I'm pining.' All that is behind it now, it goes in the car everyday to fetch my granddaughter from school. All the other children adore it. If I drive past their garden on a tractor it's always loose out there, and comes to the fence barking at me, as if to say 'This is my home and I'm in charge of it.' The sheepdog goes down to play with it and as happy endings go, this has got to be a really good one. The first morning after we dropped it off, my son came into the kitchen. The first question on everyone's lips, 'How's the dog settling in?' He says that he left the house to go to milk at 4.30am. As he went through the door the dog slipped out between his legs. 'I caught it again at half-past five.'

★★★

Married life! Last night I went upstairs for my customary pre-pub shower and shave. When I came back down my wife is sitting in her usual place on the settee. I ask her if I can have the daily paper. She says, 'I'm reading it.' So I ask her if I can have the magazine that accompanies it. 'I'm reading that next.' 'Well can I have the TV remote control?' 'I'm watching this programme.' It's all very well talking about equality of the sexes, but we've never had it around here.

28 May 2016

I had a letter from a reader called Johnny Alston (he omitted his address so I can't reply to him), and he was telling me of an experience 76 years ago. On holiday, near Bournemouth, he became aware of a meadow where hundreds of lapwings were nesting. Seeing the whole flock in distress one day he found five badgers decimating the eggs and nests. At the end of his week's holiday there wasn't a chick or egg left. His question to me: how many birds, bumble bees and hedgehogs have badgers killed since then? Millions I expect but I also expect we'd rather not know.

★★★

My life has undergone huge recent change. I'll explain. About nine months ago I swapped my car for two vehicles. I bought a 4x4 because I can't walk much anymore and I need to get around the fields, and I bought an old car for when I wanted to go 'somewhere'. The car was immaculate, it would pass for new except for the mileage, which was over 200,000. I thought it would do because I wouldn't use it much, and with any luck it would keep going. I bought it off a friend in the car trade, and the other day he asked me how it was going and how many miles I'd done. (It's a brave man who sells you a car with that on the clock and asks how it's going.) I'd got no idea what miles I'd done so I had a look. Another 10,000 miles! I couldn't believe it, so how ever did I do all those?

Then I thought of my number two grandson. It's not long until he turned 19, but he's been in no rush to pass his driving test. He's failed two tests but there have been months and months between, and I've been his unpaid taxi driver. To be fair to him, public transport is almost non-existent around here and that alone should be motivation to pass your test. And there's a car here for him: his elder brother's first car has been hanging about the yard, ready for him. So for a long time we've been having these conversations: 'Could you take me to work for 6.30 in the morning please?' (He's on a gap year and life saves at the local pool, which is six miles away.) And I've said that of course I could. On the way there he's asked if I can fetch him back at 3.30. When I'm fetching him back he says, 'Can you take me to rugby training tonight?' Rugby is 14 miles away. I say yes, and he says 'Can you fetch me back at 10.30?' There's a month or so in the spring that is quite difficult, because there's rugby on Saturday afternoons, soccer on Sunday mornings and cricket on Sunday afternoons. And you never knew where you had to fetch him from on Sunday mornings because you never knew where he would crash out on Saturday nights. Apparently crashing out on Saturday nights is cool. So for nearly two years he's been like a little bird that's standing on the edge of his nest. He's fully fledged, got all his feathers, but he's not yet taken the big step that will launch him into the outside world.

But it's third time lucky: he's just passed his test. And that's why my life has changed. He goes off with whatever bag is appropriate over his shoulder without a backward glance at me. I miss driving him about. I feel dumped. He's gone to Newquay for the weekend. Never asked me.

★★★

Most people around here have a jaundiced view of health and safety. Jaundiced seems an appropriate description given that the badge of health and safety is a yellow jacket. It's all very well poking fun at health and safety until someone gets hurt. But you will never ever legislate for everything that goes wrong. And legislation will never keep pace with man's ability to contrive an accident. I tend to be on the cautious side. But I know people who have a cavalier attitude to it all. I know, for example, people whose remedy for the fuse that keeps blowing in the plug of a welder, is to remove the fuse and replace it with a piece cut from a six inch nail!

Today's example of cavalier attitude concerns a man who was painting the steelwork of a farm building in the red oxide paint that is traditionally used for that purpose. He was about 15 feet in the air, standing in one of those one ton wooden potato boxes. The potato box was sitting on the pallet tines of a loader. Trouble is, the box just sits there, it isn't fixed on. The box falls off and tumbles to the ground as does the occupant. Fortunately he isn't hurt, apart from a few bruises. Less fortunate is the fact that the large bucket of red oxide paint lands on top of him. And he is plastered in the stuff. He cleans himself up as best he can. Over the next two days he has about eight baths and showers but there's still lots of paint on him. His mother had to remove what's left: she uses oven cleaner.

4 June 2016

Last week salt was good for you, this week you can eat as much fatty food as you like. Would it not be very handy if someone produced a diary that predicted, in advance, when these different things would be good for you. If you knew in advance you could stock up on these different foods when they were on special offer.

★★★

There's a farming family near here that are very special friends. It's not the sort of thing you do, put your friends in a sort of numerical order, or have A-list friends and B-list friends and so on. It's the sort of thing you did at school. 'He's my best friend and he's my second-best friend.' It was an order that could change as often as you changed your socks. But these are special friends to all of our family and, I'm sure, we to theirs. If you need help or need to borrow something, nothing is too much trouble, and if they can help they will. The father is halfway between my age and my son's age so I played rugby with him and so did my son David. He's godfather to my eldest grandson, Rhys, and so the connections go on. Anyway they've just had their first grandchild, a little boy. And I'm despatched with greetings cards for new grandparents and parents. And I bought a pair of wellies for the little boy. I like buying little boys their first wellies. When Rhys was born I bought his. I went in the shop and asked for some wellies for a little boy. The lady brought a pair and I said I thought they were too big. 'How old is he?' 'Two' 'They should be OK.' 'Two days' I said. She looked at me as if I were mad. I like it when folks think I'm mad, but eccentric is a kinder word.

★★★

I'm an observer of life. I like to melt into the background and to watch what's going on. Yesterday I melted into the background in the dentist's waiting room so effectively that I missed my slot because they didn't know I was there. (And someone scratched my car while I was waiting!) I watch the farmers in the pub. Sundays and Thursdays are farmers' nights. There's usually five or six of us who farm or work on farms. It's quite possible that none of us have been that far from home since our last visit to the pub. Perhaps all we've seen are our immediate family and the inside of the tractor cab. These visits to the pub are an important time to catch up. We talk of farming matters, the weather and local gossip. Mostly it's local gossip. There is a certain status accorded to the person who brings in information that the others don't know. Timing is critical here to have full impact. Go too soon and the big audience might not have arrived. Leave it too late and someone else may turn up with the same story and your place in the limelight is gone.

Someone volunteers that a local farmer was dehorning calves. A calf nearly escaped his grasp and so he put the red hot iron in his jacket pocket whilst he restrained it, and set his jacket on fire.

This anecdote doesn't have the impact the teller was hoping for. The same farmer has set his jacket on fire the two previous years and in all probability will do it again by the same method next year. A latecomer arrives, gets his pint, and joins us. He takes a long pull on his pint and starts to roll a cigarette, which usually takes him a quarter of an hour. 'I hear that Trevor who lives on the end of the hill has died.' This causes immediate impact. One of our group thinks the information is wrong. 'No he hasn't died, it's Trevor who drives the bus who has died.' The rest of us have heard neither story so we can't take a vote on it. The conversation, for the rest of us, moves on. But for the two combatants, for combatants they are, the argument is not ended. As the evening progresses various locals arrive and at each entrance the two combatants seek endorsement about who has actually died. As soon as the bar door opens, no matter what the conversation, they break off, 'Hey, have you heard that Trevor off the hill (or Trevor off the bus) has died?' As the evening progresses a clearer picture emerges. Turns out that they are both dead. A sort of equilibrium is restored. This is a good thing, credibility is restored, honours are even. Not that I'm much bothered as I didn't know either of the deceased. We make our various ways home. After initial tensions it's a happy ending of sorts. Apart from, that is, for the two Trevors.

11 JUNE 2016

Just so you should know what it's like to be a farmer, we have a 32 acre block of land which is grazed by our cows every year. There's a hardly ever used council road runs through the middle of it, it's in three fields and there are gates on the road. My son has the three fields divided up by semi-permanent electric fencing so that the cows have nice fresh grass every day. He goes to fetch the cows early on the Sunday morning of the bank holiday weekend and someone has left the gates all open and there are 30 young cattle of my neighbours in with our cows. They have strolled about in the night and completely wrecked the electric fencing. He takes all the cattle home and has to sort the visitors from our cows on his own. My neighbour, who has no help and works such long hours you wouldn't believe, spends all Sunday morning taking his cattle home in a trailer. He can't walk them home because our cows are back down the fields and they would all get mixed up again. My son and eldest grandson spend all the hours between milkings on the bank holiday Monday, repairing the electric fencing. The trouble is you will never know who left the gates open so that you can thank them personally.

★★★

I was sitting in the bathroom this week when I dropped the toilet roll, which rolled away to the door. And I sat there contemplating my predicament. I didn't have an adorable yellow Labrador puppy with me to retrieve it. For some reason my first thought was, 'this sort of thing didn't happen when you had squares of torn up newspaper stuck on a nail on the door.' And I thought about this some more. If you went back to using squares of newspaper, all the energy and resources that go in to producing an endless supply of soft toilet tissue would be saved. And the newspaper industry decline, in the face of electronic competition, would be halted and then start to grow back to historic levels. Because you would have to have a newspaper because you would need one to rip up. It's all so obvious and such a green solution. It doesn't stop there, it should become compulsory to wrap all fish and chips and takeaway meals in newspaper as well. The more I think about it, the more I think I have hit on an idea that will save the newspaper industry, not just as we know it, but more importantly, as we *knew* it. And if there is a problem, I can't think of a greener solution. In the meantime, I wonder if we could have 'square' rolls that don't roll.

★★★

Life is often about making assumptions. Some of the assumptions we make are quite critical, more critical than we think. As an example, when you are waiting at a junction in your car and there is a vehicle approaching from your right and that vehicle is indicating that it is to turn in to the road where you are, you invariably pull out. But you are assuming that the other vehicle is to turn left because that is what he is indicating. But he may have no intention of turning left, for all you know he is on one of those whiplash scams. He might be intending to drive right into you. And when he does it's only your word against his. That's an assumption of the sort we have to make every day.

Assumptions on the road have a similarity with the flea beetle. Over the last two years flea beetles have written off a field of newly sown kale, twice. As dilemmas go, that is quite a big one. We've got kale again in the same field this year. I can't afford for the flea beetle to win this year's battle. So I've made an assumption. I've assumed that if the beetles ate the kale seedlings last year and they ate them the year before that, then there is a fair chance that they are still there. I know nothing of the lifecycle of the flea beetle, I don't know if it's the same beetles there every year or if it's their successors. But I'm making the assumption that there are flea beetles there. And I've done a sort of pre-emptive strike. I've drilled the kale and just as the first few plants have shown through, I've sprayed the field with insecticide, because as recent experience has shown, if I spray the field when I see the beetles, it's much too late. They can clear a field of its seedlings in 24 hours. It seems to be working. Well it was working yesterday, I haven't been up there yet today.

There's another dilemma. We want to do our silage this week and we need dry weather for that. At the same time I have 40 acres of fodder beet and nine acres of kale that would benefit if they had a drink every day. It's a conflict I can do nothing about and over which I have no influence. I'll just have to see what happens. If the weather doesn't suit what's going on in one field, it will be OK in the next.

18 JUNE 2016

It goes from bad to worse. I told you last time that my son and grandson spent all of bank holiday Monday repairing electric fencing because someone had left a gate open and a neighbour's cattle had been on the rampage. They had to do it all again on the Thursday. This time the gate wasn't just left open, it was taken off its hinges and thrown in the nettles.

★★★

When I go to a social function and I'm watching people, I marvel at the way that some people 'work the room'. During the time they are there, they make it their business to spend a little time with absolutely everyone. They drift from one little group to the other and although they pretend to show interest in those they are presently talking to, they are also planning their next move. This is an admirable way to behave: you are someone's guest and you have a duty to talk to, and spend some time with all their other guests.

Although I admire their social prowess, I do none of it myself. I look for a seat against a wall, preferably a corner. I like to have a wall behind me. When you have had the sort of tough life I've had you are always wary of someone creeping up behind you. And I just sit there. If someone wants to talk to me that's OK, but they have to come over.

I see the 'circulators' looking at me over people's shoulders, wondering if they should come across, invariably they think better of it. I think that I can read their thoughts. They are thinking, 'He looks a miserable old sod'. And they are dead right. But plenty of people who know me come across.

Anyway I'm sitting in the corner at one such function and a lad I know comes across for a chat. He tells me that his parents are very big on feeding the birds in their garden. They spend a small fortune on bird food and bird feeders and their garden is a sort of avian paradise. It is a magnet for birds and unfortunately it has become a magnet for grey squirrels. The ingenuity of the squirrels in successfully robbing the bird feeders was very annoying. But when the squirrels turned their attentions to the birds' nests, taking eggs and babies, they went too far. His dad went out and bought an airgun, and now his mother spends a lot of time in a bedroom, popping away at squirrels. (We should all have a go at grey squirrels and our grandchildren might see some red ones!) He tells me a lot about this airgun, how sophisticated it is, and how powerful. It has its own compressed air supply so you don't have to lever it for your next shot, it is very silent and it has telescopic sights.

He goes on to tell me that if his parents are out in the evening, he goes up to the bedroom where the airgun is, and gets it out. That its range covers the gardens of three houses each side of where he lives. And if there's not much on TV he quite likes to spend an hour or so shooting the clothes pegs on neighbours' washing lines. And if a garment has two pegs holding it on the line, such is the accuracy of the airgun that he can destroy the two pegs in quick succession and the garment falls to the floor. He hasn't said so but I think we are talking about under-garments here, but then again that could just be me and my imagination. His little diversion only lasts about a week and he is found out. He seems a bit surprised at this. But if you have seven houses in a row and six of them keep finding knickers in the vegetable patch and the middle house has washing out that gets away unscathed, it's a bit of a giveaway as to where the trouble is coming from, isn't it? You don't need a degree in detective work to work that one out. He says he is going to get another drink and I ask him to bring me one, and some food as well whilst he is at it. I don't want to lose this good seat.

He's only gone a second and a young lady takes his seat. I've never met her but I know who she is and where she comes from. I miss my late mother-in-law at times like this. There was a time when I'd been out and I would tell her next day who was there and because she knew everyone for miles she would give me their pedigree going back three or four generations. Anyway, I'm having a good chat with this young lady and we are getting to know each other. She decides to tell me that she has recently been to a family wedding. She goes on to say that there were three fairly serious fights at this wedding, one in the church and two at the reception. I've never been to a wedding like that. You wouldn't have to be sponsored by a glossy magazine. You could sell tickets for a wedding like that.

25 June 2016

I'm not a garden sort of person. I can appreciate a nice garden but planting flowers and weeding is not for me. But I know that getting a nice garden doesn't just happen on its own and so I keep the lawns tidy. Keeping the lawns tidy requires a bit of effort. The grandsons sometimes venture forth on my ride on mower, and when they finish, the grass is cut, but the lawns don't look tidy. It was after one of their efforts that I took time to tidy it all up a bit. I even got some nice stripes on the main lawn, which isn't that easy with a ride-on mower.

As I finished, my wife was out putting some washing on the line. I was expecting a compliment but I didn't get one. Should have known better. Me: 'That looks nice.' 'Pity you didn't cut closer to the edges,' she says. There's two issues now with that. All along the front lawn is a wall dividing it from the field. It has one of those walls they probably called a 'ha-ha'. The top of the wall is level with the lawn and there's a drop down into the field. The wall has mostly fallen down now and stock are kept out of the garden (sometimes) with two strands of barbed wire, but the drop is still there. A couple of years ago on my travels, I met two men who had each driven a ride-on mower off such a wall, it was not an experience that they recommended or wanted to repeat. The other issue is that we've been married for over 50 years and I know for a fact that during that time she hasn't cut a single lawn. So how come she knows more about it than me?

It reminds me a bit of my brother. Every time I stay the night, he shows me this liquidiser thingy that his wife bought him. He thinks I should have one so that I can adopt a healthier lifestyle, like his. Into this liquidiser go fruit and vegetables and the resultant mix looks varying degrees of terrible, depending on how green it is. So how come he lives a healthier life than I do, if my cholesterol is 3.1 and his is about 6.5? I'll tell you why. His local shop will apparently only sell you a morning newspaper if at the same time you buy a foot-long baguette that is full of bacon, mushrooms, eggs and tomatoes. I think that you eat that baguette before you get home, I don't think you shove it in the liquidiser. When you get home, I expect you get some kitchen tissue to wipe the grease from around your mouth, then you wash the baguette down with a couple of swigs out of the liquidiser. Stable doors and bolted horses come to mind.

9 JULY 2016

On the Friday before Father's Day a strange-looking parcel appeared on our kitchen table. My wife told me what it was for and said 'Aren't you going to open it?' I said, 'But it's not due to be opened until Sunday.' 'You've got to open it today, it's alive.' So I opened it and it contained two live goldfish. Not the handiest of things to wrap up, two goldfish, but there was some water in there with them as well. Bit of a tradition in our house, goldfish.

It all started when the children were small. One year they won three at the fair. They lived for the first three years we had them in a conventional goldfish bowl in the kitchen. I was looking at them one day and I thought, that's not much of a life. They were just stuck there, nowhere to go, nothing to interest them, not much going on in their lives. A bit like my own life really. Out in the cow yard we have this concrete tank. Apparently it started life in the Second World War, it was used when everything was scarce, it was filled with straw and the straw was soaked with caustic soda which broke the straw down and made it into more digestible cattle feed. The tank is about 12 feet long, three feet deep and two feet wide (presumably it's OK to use imperial measures after the vote). We've converted it into a cow drinking trough, for which purpose it is admirable, it holds lots of water and lots of cows can get around it to drink at the same time.

And that's where I put the three goldfish, and they flourished. Someone once told me that goldfish will grow to a size that is in proportion to the environment in which they live. For three years in their bowl they had stayed the same size they had arrived at, about two inches. Two years after that they were six inches long. We never fed them. When cows went for a drink they would gather around and pick fragments of food off the hairs around the cows' muzzle. Nothing lasts forever and after about ten years they died down to one fish. In really cold spells the tank froze almost solid, but they had survived. The last lone fish grew to about a foot long. I found him one day dead on the concrete: he must have got over excited and jumped clear out of the tank. There's three new ones in the tank now, they are about six inches long. These two newer ones have gone into a smaller tank, don't know enough about goldfish to know if they are cannibals or not. I'll let them grow a bit before they join the others.

★★★

If there's one thing that my wife and I don't agree on, it's shopping. She loves it, I avoid it at all costs. She goes shopping every day, once a year would be enough for me. If we go away for a three day break, which we try to do twice a year, she usually thinks that she needs about 12 presents to take home with her. But she doesn't buy them all in one go, she drags it out to about four a day. Even though it means revisiting the same shops two or three times. I never ever go into the shop with her when she is at these purchasing deliberations but I do admit that if there is a charity shop handy I will go in there to see if there are any books that I fancy or something really cheap to wear. A lot of my working clothes come from charity shops, and I've got a really expensive heavy overcoat that must have cost £500 but cost me £15, I save this for rural funerals in the winter.

This latest incident happened because of her car. It's a dilemma that most of us have at some time. Her car is worth about £250 when it's going OK. But it isn't going OK, it needs about £500 spending on the gearbox and £500 on the suspension. The dilemma is that after you spend the £1,000, it's still only worth £250. And therefore if you spend £1,000, and something else goes wrong, you have to spend even more because how else will you get your £1,000 back? I'm sure you follow me on this. But I've got a friend in the motor trade and he says he will have a good look at her car and lend her one to go on with, and he will also see if he can find her a replacement for the same money. Here comes my master stroke. She says she will come with me for a ride when I swap the cars over. This is wifely speak for, 'I think I'll pop to the shops on the way back.' The appointed time comes and she says, 'Surely you are not going dressed like that?' I'm in my warm weather working gear. I'm wearing a fairly tatty short-sleeved shirt, but what she really finds objectionable is the shorts, and with them I am wearing a pair of very heavy, dirty, working boots and a pair of thick socks, the sort you wear inside your wellies, these come halfway up my legs. It is quite clear that she is ashamed to be out with me, which is good. Because, when on the way back, she says that she just wants to pop in the shops, there is no way that she wants me to go in with her, in fact she seems quite pleased that I don't park too near.

16 JULY 2016

I am often minded of the time when I took a good friend for a ride around the farm. OK, it was the man who publishes my books. (Not everyone has a publisher, so I might as well flaunt it a bit.) He knows a lot about nature and loves it, as do I. And he says, as we drive the mile or so to the land we rent, 'I often think that you exaggerate when you write about the numbers of predators that are about.' As it happened, it was the day after we had finished our silage. Freshly-cleared grass fields are like a magnet for birds. There's all sort of food available to them, stuff that has been killed by the mower or harvester and the grubs and worms are so much more accessible.

We went into one cleared field and he counted 15 buzzards, which amazed him. But that was as nothing to the next field. On the next field there were buzzards everywhere. I stopped the truck and he counted 57! I was particularly reminded of that incident quite recently. Stephen was out mowing and I went to see how he was getting on. I didn't know which field he would be in and there is nowhere where you can park and see all the fields in order to locate him. When I got to the rented land, I stopped and lowered the windows, perhaps I could hear him.

But I didn't need to hear him. On the horizon there was a scene that was just like the scene you see in a wildlife documentary in Africa. Or better still, in a Western film. In either case there would have to be a dead body. In the former case it could be the result of a lion kill, in the Western film, a dead horse or human victim of some violence. What I could see on the horizon was the unmistakable flight pattern of birds of prey, circling about. Circling about like vultures.

I went to the field where they were and sure enough there was Stephen with the mower. He stopped for a chat, and we counted 27 red kites either on or flying over the 15 acre field. Stephen had carried three little leverets to the safety of the hedgerow but he had seen five others carried off by the kites. The kite story is one of huge success but when does success become a plague? You could argue that we were to blame for the leverets' predicament because if we hadn't been mowing, the leverets would have been safer. But that would imply that we shouldn't farm and that wildlife should come first. And I know that there are plenty of people who think that is just how it should be.

★★★

23 July 2016

Farmers have to do what they call 'greening' to a percentage of temporary grass and cereal acreage (I can never remember if it's 3% or 5% but I made sure I knew when I worked it out.) Farmers put in a range of options that are designed to help wildlife and the environment. I chose a combination of field margins, which I left to form wildlife corridors, and areas of fallow. The areas altogether were sown to stubble turnips. These were grazed in December and the ground left untouched until the first of July. By the time we get to 1st July the fallow is full of what farmers call 'filth'. It's a three-foot high jungle of weeds and weed grasses. I've been out this week with what we call a topper, chopping it all off. But filth is not all it's full of. It's full of skulking cock pheasants, who are keeping a low profile as they change their plumage and hares that seem as big as sheep. As you can imagine, the sight of these latter, makes my day.

★★★

Yesterday when my wife told me how many days there were left until Christmas, I pretended to be interested. 'Is that all, I must get six turkeys for Christmas dinner.'

Regular readers will know that turkeys are a contentious issue here. My last little turkey flock terrorised the yard. People couldn't get out of the house, couldn't get into their cars, and if they did they couldn't get out again. 'We can buy a perfectly good turkey from the butchers.' 'Ah but your own turkey, off your own yard, tastes so much better.' 'Why do you need six?' 'The fox will probably want four or five.' I can see she's thinking about this, because she knows full well that if I am so minded, a flock of turkeys will suddenly appear. But I don't give her any respite, I go for my next hit. My old dog Mert is showing his age now. He lives outside the back door which is where I feed him. He doesn't go far. He goes out into the garden to perform his ablutions which he does where the B&B guests park their cars. We don't do picking up dog poo on this farm, we just spread it about with the lawn mower (which is much, much better than getting it in your strimmer).

Mert doesn't come for rides in my truck anymore and he knows I miss him. She also suspects that when the day finally comes, I will replace him. 'I'm thinking about buying a new puppy dog.' 'You can't while Mert is still alive, it would upset him.' 'Every successful business should have a succession policy in place.' 'It's not coming in the house.' 'Yes it is, it will guard against burglars.' 'What sort of dog do you want?' 'A Rottweiler or German shepherd.' She goes very quiet now and I can see that she is thinking. I think I have a good idea what she is thinking. She's not thinking about Christmas. The tree and the lights have gone back into the attic and the holly has gone back on the tree. She's thinking about being attacked by vicious stag turkeys when she's putting the washing out. She's thinking of half-grown puppy dogs destroying her furniture because grandsons have left the kitchen door open into the living room, all night. She's thinking of puddles of dog pee all over the kitchen floor when she gets up in the morning. But it turns out that's not what she's thinking at all, I've got that completely wrong. 'There's no point in you getting a puppy at your age, it will outlive you, you need to get an oldish rescue dog.' She's turned the tables on me in no time at all. Now it's me that goes quiet. It's me that's doing all the thinking.

30 July 2016

The trouble with exercise in the home, is that it is really boring. When I was regularly playing rugby I had, at different times, an exercise bike and a rowing machine in my bedroom. The novelty of these soon wore off and they both became the place to hang your clothes. This was considered marginally better than throwing them on the floor, which I otherwise do. In fact there are few better places to hang your shirts than the handlebars of an exercise bike. Rather than spend half an hour exercising in the comfort of my home I much preferred to drive 15 miles to play two hours of violent indoor football (I still have marks on my shins to remind me).

I have reached the stage in my life when I have to do exercise again to try to preserve my mobility. I can do a lot of stuff at home but it's still as boring as it ever was. The doctor has referred me to the local gym. Never been to a gym before, not a modern gym anyway. When I go the first time I have to do what they call an induction. I am under the guidance of a lovely girl who happens to be married to one of my nephews, which makes her a sort of relative, a sort of aunty I think. She and I have a lot in common, we are both too nice to have married into this family. The induction is partly just that and partly family gossip. Part of the serious bit is to ask me if I've ever had any operations, what they were and when.

Without having to think I said I'd had my appendix out on 1964 and a hernia operation in the winter of 1971.

A hernia operation is no big deal. The danger for a farmer is that he undoes it all by lifting something before it is properly healed. I had mine in January, the theory was that I wouldn't need to catch any sheep before lambing at the end of March, so what turns up? Only one of the coldest winters ever. We had minus 25 around here. Diesel froze in tractors, milk was freezing in the pipeline before you had finished milking! At home here all I had was a 16-year-old employee who was helped by my 14-year-old son. They did really well in the circumstances. One day, in hospital, I put my jug of water outside the window. When I got it back in after half an hour there was an inch of ice on it. When the matron came round she asked if we were warm enough. I said I was cold. She said it felt quite warm. I showed her the ice on my water jug. She wasn't a fun matron, she was like a very nasty sergeant major in drag. She summoned the very harassed boiler man, showed him the ice and gave him a fearful bollocking. Still feel a bit guilty about that.

6 August 2016

I knew it was a mistake as soon as I went in there. I'd been away for the day visiting friends and I got back in home territory by early evening. I knew there would be no one at home. Besides that, I was busting to go to the loo and when you are busting for the loo, two more miles can make a lot of difference. So I thought I'd call in the pub on the way home. It may be the same pub, my local, but at a different time of day it can be very different. Because at different times of day you get a very different clientele.

There were only two people in there. One was a very good friend of mine, he has a small hill farm about three miles away. Seven days a week he is in the pub by 7 o'clock (his wife drops him off) and he's still there at closing time, at whatever time that might be. The other person there was a very big, very loud man.

He is doing all the talking, very loud talking. I slip into a seat in the corner and listen. I say listen, but I'm not paying any attention, because the talk is a sort of background noise, a bit like what they call piped music. I can see that my friend isn't listening either, he's puffing contentedly on his pipe and has a faraway look in his eyes. Sometimes when he's puffing on his pipe his eyes are so far away that I wonder what he's actually smoking. He shouldn't be smoking anyway, but the landlord is not too bothered when it's quiet, and after all, he is his best customer.

I turn my attention to the speaker, who takes this as a sign that I'm actually listening to him and is thus encouraged. But I'm not listening at all, I'm imagining him fitting neatly in to a bygone era. I can imagine him as some sort of colonial policeman in an immaculate khaki uniform with shorts that come down below his knees and he's sure to be carrying a stick. I can see him in the era when a lot of the world's map was pink. I can remember when I was at school the teachers would indicate a map of the world and say 'all the pink countries are ours'. As if to reinforce the colonial theme, he empties his glass and says, 'Just time for one more sundowner.'

When we first started doing bed and breakfast, the very first guests we had were a lovely South African couple. They asked Ann and me if we would like to join them for a 'sundowner,' and would we bring four glasses and a jug of water into the lounge. So we sat there for an hour having a good chat and the South Africans kept looking out of the window to where the sun was making its slow journey behind the hills at the other side of our valley. I've been to South Africa and the sun sets so quickly there, you can almost see it move. They got fed up with waiting in the end and opened the bottle of Scotch they had, sun down or not.

13 August 2016

The threat of TB is never far from your mind. It's all about you. It crops up in the conversations in the pub on a regular basis. As one of your friends goes clear, so another's herd goes down. And as going clear involves having two consecutive, clear, 60-day tests, there is always someone in the locality involved in testing. We have been clear of TB for several years now. In that time we have only brought one animal onto the farm, a bull, and our cattle don't have any contact with any neighbours' cattle. Where they could come near to neighbours' cattle, we have established wildlife margins along the boundary that keep them apart.

The big worry, when you are clear, is the annual 12 monthly TB test. But you can easily forget that there are other tests along the way. Every time that you send an old cow off to slaughter at the end of her working life, she is examined for TB at the abattoir. We sent off one such cow a few weeks ago and were appalled that lesions were found in her. She isn't a definite fail but a culture is being grown on the affected parts and we've not heard the results yet. With our annual test now due, this is not a good omen.

As omens go it proved to be accurate. One in-calf heifer failed the test. What a waste, she was due to have her first calf in six weeks' time. She has already gone for slaughter, we will get just over £600 for her. A heifer of the same quality would cost over £1000, even in these depressed times.

The repercussions for this farm are endless. Best-case scenario is that we have two clear 60-day tests. That's four months before we can sell any calves. So all the calves we usually sell, we will have to find food for, room for, and we will miss the revenue. One way to avoid some of these issues is to slaughter the calves at birth. We've never done that and it's a solution we don't wish to contemplate.

The really frustrating aspect of this whole sorry mess, and I mean really frustrating, is that there is nothing we could have done to avoid all this, we just have to bear the trouble, the anguish and the cost. Some will say that we should keep our cattle in the buildings all the year round, and wildlife-proof the buildings. But all the evidence suggests that that is not what consumers want: they want to see cattle outside, eating grass, and quite rightly so.

All this is just when things were starting to look more promising. The price of our chickens is starting to creep back up. The headlong decline of milk prices looks to have reached the bottom, probably due to a decline in milk production, which in turn is probably due to farmers ceasing production and other farmers slaughtering cows. Just when things were on the move up, something like a TB failure turns up to drag you back down.

But then farming was ever thus. The long-awaited journey to an effective policy that will deliver some progress on all this is in the hands of politicians. In this high-tech era it should be quite easy to add up just how many cattle are slaughtered every year on the TB sacrificial altar. I think it's over 30,000. How many football pitches would they fill? Only with a visual impression of the scale of what is going on, would people grasp the true enormity of it all.

★★★

Returning to my theory of how different sets of people have different times when they go to the pub – this can loosely be described as the early evening crowd and the late evening crowd. There are some folk that don't fit either category but that is the general way of things. A lot of people turn up within five minutes of their regular time. If I go to the pub I always go at 9pm, that gets me to the pub at five past. But it sometimes comes to pass that a person who goes out at 6.30 to 7, instead of going home after a couple of hours, finds himself delayed unexpectedly during sort of limbo hour between 8.30 and 9.30. And there's new company arriving, so why go home? And after being there, perhaps four hours, and getting a bit full of beer, the obvious remedy is a journey across the optics on the top shelf. So what if it is midnight? They've had a good evening. And they make their way home. It's not an easy walk across the village but they always seem to make it, often with the aid of fellow travellers who have had less to drink. Persons thus afflicted often adopt a gait whereby their left leg seems to be trying to walk where their right leg should be, and vice versa. This phenomenon is known locally as plaiting your legs. But there are repercussions: they don't get away unscathed. I asked my grandsons (who visit licensed premises most days), if they had seen old Fred about lately for he had recently indulged himself in one of these adventures. 'No, he's still under house arrest.'

20 AUGUST 2016

Today we address the issue of stupidity. The Lynx UK Trust have already earmarked the Keilder Forest and adjacent Scottish border area as their preferred site for a 'Lynx' trial. Norwegian experts tell us that 400 Lynx will kill 4,000 sheep a year and that compensation to farmers will amount to £560,000 a year. So that's OK then. No one seems to have asked the sheep what they think. In a nation that agonised about culling TB-infected badgers, and probably people who support Lynx reintroduction are at the forefront of that group, the obviously confused thinking is bizarre. I move quickly on. I was listening to a programme on the radio about wolves, it was very interesting and touched on the place of the wolf in folklore. One of the wolf experts clearly thought that the time had come to reintroduce the wolf to the UK. He was asked what would happen to the sheep. And again I quote, 'There is only a problem with sheep because the wolf has been extinct in this country for so long that farmers have forgotten how to look after their sheep properly.' You have to think that statement through.

By saying that sheep are not looked after properly, we can only assume he means that all sheep should be put into safe sheds at night. And if he means that, it means that your wolf who was hungry at night is still hungry in the morning and therefore the farmer has to stand in the fields all day to protect his sheep. And if the farmer looks after his sheep in a manner that he describes as 'properly', and the wolf can't get at the sheep, what will the wolf eat? Children? How long before a hungry pack of wolves discover that there are rich pickings to be had around the chimes of an ice cream van? The only safe thing to assume is that he has no idea what he means. Comparisons were made with the reintroduction of wolves to the Yellowstone National Park in the USA. How you can compare that vast area to a small island with over 60 million people is beyond me. The naivety displayed when talking about food production is so breathtaking, it's scary.

★★★

Enough of this seriousness. I didn't tell you that I was going on holiday, did I? A relative had to cancel a holiday on Crete at short notice so I had eight days there for the cost of the flights. I went with my brother; I didn't take my wife, I couldn't afford for both of us to go. If I go anywhere with my brother he agonises that people will think we are gay, but I probably shouldn't say that, it's probably not PC. Crete, at this time of year, is as hot as anywhere I've ever been to. I got quite sunburnt, not a pretty sight. I was in a tavern one night and a man at the next table who was looking at the menu, looked at me, and said, 'I'll have the lobster.'

My wife likes to buy lots of presents when she's on holiday, I prefer to buy none. But I like to have a quiet life, so I bought her a purse and a bracelet. She unwrapped them; I can spot lukewarm when I see it. 'Ah,' I said, 'but your big present is to come by post.' 'What have you bought me?' 'I've bought you one of those long black dresses and a black shawl like those Greek widow ladies wear.' Big mistake.

27 August 2016

Down at the 'gym', for people like me (and probably you), who like watching people, there is much to see. I go there because both my knees are worn out. I played rugby regularly until I was 50, in the front row. I pulled tug-of-war for ten years, which probably didn't help, but I suspect that the biggest factor is a lifetime spent paddling about on concrete, in wellies, milking cows. The theory is that if I exercise my leg muscles, they will tighten up my knee joints. If I was a machine they would probably put some washers in there to take up the slack. I'm sure that with hindsight the Almighty looks down on what He creates and regrets that he didn't fit grease nipples to people's knees and hips. It has gone unsaid, but not unnoticed, that because of other health issues I have, it's not worth fitting me with new knees. But we are where we are, I don't dwell on it, and where we are is down the gym.

The first thing that strikes you are the fashion statements. People you are used to seeing in the street are wearing completely different outfits here. I won't go into detail of what the ladies are wearing, because that would make me appear some sort of voyeur (which I probably am but there's no need to make it official). Suffice to say that the younger ladies wear outfits like you see on TV on these adverts for keep fit videos. And as the ladies get older it gets a bit more casual. The men under 40 wear something that is clearly contrived to make them look hard, and over 40 and they want to look nonchalant. Me, I wear whatever I happen to be wearing when it is time to go. The only concession I make is to change out of my dirty work boots. But there is one fashion accessory they all have, a bottle of water. They clutch it to their bosoms or chests as they move from apparatus to apparatus as if this bottle were the very essence of life itself. All except me. The instructors who also carry bottles of water and are very caring, they often offer to fetch me a bottle from the machine. 'Can I fetch you a bottle of water?' 'Nah.' Never bought one and never will, though I am toying with the idea of taking a carton of milk in there with me, which as we all know is much cheaper.

The men that are aged in their twenties are all trying to look macho as are the men in their seventies. As are all the men in the age groups inbetween. I do most of my watching from the exercise bike. It is a much loved tactic of the instructors to put you on a bike and programme it for 15 minutes whilst they go to the loo, for a cup of coffee or whatever. I don't find it too onerous, pedalling away on a bike, I usually crank up the degree of difficulty when they are not looking: might as well work hard whilst I'm here. To my left is a man doing very fast walking on one of those things that go round and round (hang on a minute, here's a grandson: it's called a treadmill). To be fair, he is walking really fast, and keeps it up for all of the hour I'm there. What's the point of walking hard for an hour looking at a green wall? When there are so many lovely walks around here, what's all that about?

Over at the other side of the gym are two young men lifting weights. They do it in front of big mirrors. I soon worked out that these mirrors are not aids to improving their technique, they are aids to help them to look around the gym behind them, to see if there is anyone watching. I'm watching, I'm pedalling away on my bike and they keep catching my eye. And I keep catching their eye. I'm trying to look scornful and it must be working, because they seem to redouble their efforts. I actually feel scornful, because even from here I can see that what they are lifting is all bar and not much weight. The word to use is posing, I think it comes from the French word poseur, it's an admirable word for this situation. And I do actually feel a bit scornful, because when I was their ages, what repetitive lifting I did was probably a heavy bale of hay on the end of a pike, and we didn't do it for just an hour, we had to do it all day long. That's why we never had to go to a gym to do repetitive work. All we are doing in a gym is trying to emulate hard manual labour. I'm not anti-gym, but we could all do this exercise at home, we have a ready weight available, our own body weight, and the permutations of lifting that body weight are endless, but it's true that exercising at home can be really boring. Going to the gym is a form of discipline. Once you start, you have to keep going: there might be someone watching.

PS Part of the induction when I started going to the gym involved getting weighed so I thought I would try to lose some weight while I was at it. For over 30 years I didn't take sugar in tea or coffee, then one day I was making drinks for a few of us and I got a sugary one by mistake. Mmm, I thought, that's nice, so I've had two spoonfuls in every cup for four years. I've cut that right out, for a month now. And I weighed again and I haven't lost a single ounce or put one on. What conclusions do we draw from that little experiment? None at all, except that I've saved on the cost of the sugar.

3 September 2016

I've got to work some stubble up so we can sow some stubble turnips. It's on our very highest field. I could do it in one big day but decide to do it over the weekend in two lots. I'm actually looking forward to it, it's so nice up there and I never tire of the panoramic views. So I set off, earlyish, and after I have made sure that the cultivator is working OK I look around for the birds. Any activity that involves disturbing the soil usually brings birds flocking to the scene, but it's two hours before I get three buzzards. There's a clumsiness to how they walk and how they fly that suggests they are juveniles.

Not long after the buzzards, a red kite turns up and in no time there are seven of them. The tractor gets within a length of them before they fly further on. When you get as close as that, you realise what a beautiful bird a buzzard is, and just how big. Then three lapwings turn up but theirs is only a flying visit: literally, they are there for just a few seconds. I can't tell if the buzzards and kites have scared them off but it's good to see them about.

Suddenly all the birds take off together! What's spooked them? I soon find out two hares have burst through the hedge and are careering around the stubble in what seems to be a serious fight. I can't tell if their dispute is territorial or sexual but they crash back through the hedge and are gone.

It's mid-afternoon by now and I haven't spoken to anyone

or seen anyone all day. I contemplate this for a while. It's quite a rare phenomenon in our modern lives, a bit of solitude. A bit of solitude is OK. But that soon changes: over the boundary hedge my neighbour is going around his sheep on his quad bike. He pulls up, climbs the fence, walks across the field for a chat. The chat lasts an hour, but I'm in no rush and that's fine by me. I do another hour after he's gone and then head off home. It would only take another two or three hours to finish but I enjoy being up here so much, it's nice to save a bit for tomorrow.

When I get up there the next morning the buzzards and kites are waiting for me and before long they are joined by four herring gulls who have probably stopped for a snack on their way to the seaside. When I finish I go around the outside of the field twice to erase any wheel marks and to leave the field looking tidy. This is better than a morning reading the Sunday papers. The simple pleasures of a simple farmer.

★★★

Today I bring you sad news. Everything in life is relative and this is about as sad as it gets. Mert, my faithful dog, has been run over and killed. I won't dwell on the cause of his death, only to say that it was just a few yards from our back door, where he spent most of his time. I'm sure it was an accident but there's an element of bitterness within me that his life ended in this way and with most accidents, there's often a degree of carelessness. I have never ever told people I meet that I do this bit of writing, but if they do work it out, the first thing they always say is 'How's Mert?' He became one of the best-known dogs in the West Country, and rightly so. In his memory I will tell you a 'Mert' story. I know that I've told it before but it's a favourite of mine.

I once had an old Discovery that was difficult to start. It was, mechanically, sort of OK, the problem was with the immobiliser in the key fob: sometimes it would start, sometimes it wouldn't. It therefore seemed eminently sensible that if you had got it going, you left it going until you had finished with it. Mert and I went everywhere together in it and one day I went into a local town to go to the bank. I left the Discovery parked at the side of the road with the engine running. When I returned there was a police car double parked next to it. It wasn't a little Astra like the local police use, it was a big BMW. It had big yellow stripes down the doors so the policemen knew where to get back in.

The policeman was on the pavement, and the conversation went a bit like this. 'Is this your vehicle?' 'Yes.' 'You shouldn't leave it running unattended: it's an offence.' 'I left it running because it doesn't always start.' And I told him about the key fob. He seemed a bit sympathetic to that but went on to say, 'If you leave it running like that anyone could steal it.' 'I don't think they will.' Sympathy quickly turns to impatience, 'Of course they can, the doors are open, the keys are in it and even the engine's running, everything a car thief would want, on a plate.' 'I don't think they would take it.' He's getting beyond impatience now. 'Of course they will, let's see what you've got in the back.' The windows are a bit steamed up on the inside so he puts his nose against the glass. What I've got in the back tries to bite his nose off through the glass, his teeth clink loudly and ominously, and he barks ferociously. The policeman jerks his head back and his hat comes off. 'Oh, I see what you mean.' And we go our various ways. My life used to take me away a lot, but no matter where I'd been or for how long, when I returned home, I opened the car door and Mert was there to put his head on my knee. I miss him.

10 SEPTEMBER 2016

They are back, the hare coursers are back at their evil work. The local awareness of the problem is quite high but those who do the coursing have little regard for the law and no one has caught them at their work, and if you did, what would you do about it? Keep your head down, that's what most people would do, and who can blame them. The keeper has his pheasant poults now and they are exploring their new world, so he is out quite regularly at night on fox patrol. He reports seeing 14 hares on a field we had just cleared for silage, plus several leverets. And there was mating activity going on amongst the adults. Now here's a strange thing. When coursers have been in a field (or fields), they have started leaving the dead hares near the roadside gates on show. At first this would seem like a sort of gesture, cocking a snook. It's a sort of message, 'Look what we've done,' but it's more than just that. The hares' bodies are arranged in a certain way. Always in neat rows, sometimes their backs all towards the gate, sometimes their heads, sometimes their feet. What do you reckon that's all about? Is it some sort of hare coursers' shorthand?

★★★

The management of our pub changed hands nearly two years ago. New management invariably brings change and one of the first changes was the disappearance of the juke box. We regulars weren't asked our opinion, there was no referendum. It might not seem a big deal but the juke box was quite popular. The most popular song was *Islands in the Stream*, which is a sort of village anthem. My favourite is *When You Were Sweet Sixteen* by the Fureys and I used to put it on most nights I was there. I was 16 once, but as I remember I was never sweet. We get background music now in the pub, it's played via a laptop, but it's not music we have chosen, which is what a juke box gave us. The present incumbents get regular reminders that we would like our juke box back, but to no avail. I contribute to our local parish newsletter on behalf of the parish council and I've raised the issue in there, sometimes with humour, sometimes with sarcasm. (I'm quite good at sarcasm.)

So last week the pub manager starts to relent. He says to me (his main critic) that he can play any tune in the world on his laptop and he will let me choose one tune a night, when I'm there. I tell him that I will accept his offer but just in case he changes his mind we will start on the Christmas tunes and get them out of the way. My favourite of these is *Fairytale of New York* by the Pogues. So we are sitting there, on a hot night in August listening as Kirsty MacColl sings 'and the bells are ringing out for Christmas Day.' This has made me really popular.

17 September 2016

Today you find me lost for words. To be specific, the words that I am looking for are adjectives. So what I'll do, is tell you the story and you can choose your own adjective to tack on the end of it.

I recently told you that we had made some silage on a field. What we had done was to bale the silage into large round bales and we had wrapped them in plastic. I also told you that the following night the keeper had gone foxing with his lamp and had counted 14 adult hares and some leverets on the same field. The keeper works full time on a farm a couple of miles away and at this time of year he leaves home each morning in the dark so that at the first glimmer of daylight, he can go around his pheasant pens.

A day or so later he is going around in the half light of morning and something is moving amongst the silage bales so he goes to investigate. What he finds is a big lurcher dog, abandoned by hare coursers, tied with a piece of string to one of the bales. It's a friendly dog, a dog that is very pleased to see him. He unties it and it gets onto his mule with him. (A mule is a sort of enlarged quad bike and there's lots of them around here and they should not be confused with the progeny of a cross between a horse and a donkey, which are rare.) It takes a couple of hours to do the pheasant feeding and the lurcher goes round with him the whole way and clearly enjoys the experience.

At 9 o'clock the keeper is at the vets to see if the dog is micro-chipped. As long shots go this has got to be one of the longest. People who don't tax, insure or MOT their vehicles are hardly going to bother to identify their dogs, especially if they discard them in this manner. The vets get in touch with a lurcher rescue organisation who turn up a few hours later to collect it. They say that they have had 20 lurchers in over the last month, all abandoned on farms in a similar manner. They are told that all abandoned lurchers have one thing in common, they are very friendly. If they are very friendly there's a chance they don't kill the hares to their owner's satisfaction. Some of the lurchers had been tied up for several days before they were discovered. So that's the story. The adjectives you use to describe the people who abandoned them is up to you.

★★★

To continue the doggy theme but in a happier vein. There's lots of clichés to describe what I am about to say, but I will trouble you with only one. 'Time is a great healer.' It's a month now since my dog Mert was run over and killed. Obviously I still miss him. I was backing my car out last night and without thinking I was looking in all my mirrors to make sure he wasn't in the way. But, although there's a part of me that feels a bit guilty, I am starting to think of getting a replacement. And the options are endless. There's a multitude of breeds, there's a multitude of puppies (too expensive), there's all those rescue dogs that need rescuing. One thing I am clear about is that I couldn't do with a dog that wasn't intelligent.

We sort of rescued a dog for my youngest granddaughter. As a little girl's pet it is perfect, it's a cross, can't remember what cross, it looks like a fluffy poodle. Boy, is it thick! I used to have a vet, he was a great dog lover and we often used to discuss dogs and the merits of different breeds. I have to be careful now, lest I should give offence, but I was telling him about a particular breed I liked and he said 'There's another attribute that they have: between their two ears there's nothing but solid bone.' It is obvious to me that the most intelligent breeds of dogs come from working breeds. Those are mainly sheepdogs and gundogs. What other breeds do you see sniffing around the carousel at an airport? None.

24 SEPTEMBER 2016

I start today where I finished last time, when I was discussing the intelligence of various breeds of dogs. I know that I'm on dangerous ground here, because to cast aspersions on someone's dog and its abilities can be explosive. More so than doing something similar with regard to their human relatives. It is often said that people grow to resemble their dogs, in looks. I would go further than that by saying that they resemble their dogs also in manner. It is quite obvious to most of us that some dogs don't have any common sense. It is also fairly obvious that most of their owners don't either. Why else do people let their dogs run loose in a field of sheep? Why else do people take their dogs on a lead into a field of cows and calves? But there is a mitigating factor here: how is the dog owner to know his dog doesn't have any common sense if he doesn't have any himself? It all seems quite obvious to me.

Now here's a story of a dog with an abundance of common sense. A friend of mine is decorating her room one weekend. She has a lovely little cocker spaniel and she decides that a lively cocker spaniel and open tins of paint don't mix, so it is decided that the dog will spend the day with a friend who lives in the same village. That's OK then, but halfway through the morning she gets a phone call from someone who says they have just seen her dog walking the main street in the village. 'You must be mistaken,' she says 'my dog is around at xx.' An hour later she gets an identical phone call from someone else. She phones her friend up. 'Where's my dog?' 'Out in the garden.' 'Will you just check?' 'No, she's not.' The two friends meet up and scour the village for the missing spaniel, but to no avail. 'Let's go to the pub and ask if anyone has seen her.' They go to the pub and there is the spaniel asleep on the rug in front of the fireplace. The landlord says she has been there for two hours and has been very relaxed. There's conclusions to draw from this story. The dog knew it was more likely to be reunited with its owner by going to the pub than if it went home. It clearly knew the way to the pub better than it knew the way home. It clearly goes to the pub quite a lot and it clearly has a lot of common sense.

★★★

As I write this, if I have a sixth sense, it is telling me – don't go there. But I will, I know it's a very delicate subject, but don't you sometimes tire of some of the political correctness that abounds in the world we live in? Is it not a strange phenomenon that in the digital world all around us, one of the yardsticks of life is still the pendulum, and this particular pendulum has gone too far the wrong way and needs to balance itself a bit nearer the centre? There is, near here, a troupe of Morris dancers. They are proud that their style is based on old traditions. These old traditions include wearing black top hats, adorned with feathers, and blackened faces. They tell me the black faces were originally used as a disguise when dancing was banned by the Puritans. I readily confess that I have no idea about that, but I'm sure they mean no offence and don't see themselves as some sort of latter-day Black and White Minstrel Show, with sticks and bells. Inevitably there are critics that want them to stop turning their faces black.

Years ago I had to go to an important meeting with a lady I worked with. I put my best suit on, and when I met her I could see that she had made a similar effort. I said to her, 'You look nice.' She said, 'Thank you, but you do know that you're not supposed to say that anymore.' She didn't mind what I'd said, she was quite pleased I'd noticed, it was just a bit of a warning that in an office environment, you have to be careful. Every day I check online to see if there's any news in the rugby world. A few weeks ago there was some criticism being directed towards Exeter rugby club because they called themselves Exeter Chiefs. It was suggested they should drop the word 'Chiefs' as it was likely to cause offence to the indigenous people of North America! I like watching the Chiefs on TV. I like the idea of a club that seems to have come from nowhere, getting to the top and challenging older and more established clubs.

As far as I know, the club didn't respond to this criticism.

Don't you think the time has come when 'we' should respond, or am I the only one who thinks it's all getting a bit ridiculous? Isn't it time that people stood up to the PC brigade and said 'Enough is enough, why don't you get yourself a real life?' Someone like me. At its very worst, political correctness manifests itself in the human rights of violent criminals, who deserve no rights at all.

PS I've since learned another theory as to why the faces of Morris men were blackened. To protect them from their employers, as the dancing was not approved of. Lest they be recognised and dismissed from their employment, they blackened their faces with soot from the hearth (being the most readily available material) to disguise themselves with. If they all looked the same, they couldn't be easily identified. Whatever the reason, the PC brigade have got it wrong.

1 OCTOBER 2016

I don't often write about the weather. Writing about the weather usually comes back to bite you. I might take a chance this time as we have already been bitten. Tuesday and Wednesday this week were forecast to be the hottest days in September on record, and in some places they were. We thought it would be a chance to have one of those 'big' weeks. We cut all of our third cut silage on the Monday and we thought that over the next couple of days we would gather that and the 30 acres of spring barley we still have left to do. And what happened? On the Tuesday they had those record temperatures elsewhere – whilst we had half an inch of rain. Three days later the cut grass is looking worse for wear, as is the barley and it's been so overcast and close that even the yard hasn't dried off. Still, you have to look on the bright side – yesterday I found six mushrooms.

★★★

The farmers who bring a story to the table at the pub on Thursday nights take pride in bringing a story that makes an impact. Here's one that makes an impact. This, to me. 'I hear your son-in-law has been shot.' It's news to me. I saw my son-in-law a few hours earlier and he looked fine, no mention of being shot. And I would assume that if he had, he would tell me. As far as the story-teller is concerned, my son-in-law was out in the fields and a bullet came from nowhere and grazed his hips! Next day I'm on the phone to my daughter to get more details. And the detail is very much as I've told you. 'He's here now, have a word with him.' He tells me that he was out working and a bullet grazed his hips, it didn't do too much damage but it broke the skin. He is totally unfazed by the incident – in grandchildren speak, he is really cool about it. 'Did you report it?' He says he didn't. His farm is surrounded by very high land on all sides and the shot could have come from anywhere and the person who made the shot would have no idea where it ended up or what he'd done. 'Besides I'm quite busy, I didn't want any fuss with the police and the papers.' There's laid-back for you! If you fire a rifle, the bullet can travel up to a mile and you should ascertain that there's nothing in front of you that can come to any harm. A shotgun fires lots of pellets a relatively short distance but you need a shotgun if you go shooting pheasants or if you happen to be riding as protection on a stage coach (that's why they call it riding shotgun!). After the indignation subsides you realise that he is quite right though there is obviously someone, with a rifle, somewhere, who should take a bit more care. And it doesn't bear to think about what would have happened if the bullet had landed in a different place or if there had been children about.

In a similar vein, sort of, is the story of two brothers who farmed adjoining farms. They didn't get on, they didn't get on at all, in fact they were at each other's throats at the slightest opportunity. One of the brothers had a full-time job and would leave for work at 8 o'clock every morning. As soon as he had gone, the other brother would sneak down and let his sheep into a field that his sibling had shut up for hay. He would get them out again mid-afternoon before his brother returned home from work. Every weekend the brother who owned the field would look over the gate and wonder why his hay crop wasn't growing. After two weeks he goes into the field, sees the fresh sheep poo, and soon works out what is going on. He decides to take the next week off. He gets his wife to drive the car away at the usual time and sneaks down behind the hedge to watch. Sure enough, here comes his brother gathering his sheep prior to letting them into the field to do some illicit grazing. But he has his shotgun with him and just as his brother is about to remove a hurdle from the hedge and let his sheep through, he fires a couple of warning shots over his head.

It was the village policeman who told me this story. 'I wasn't too bothered about the one brother firing shots, but when the other went home, fetched his shotgun and started firing back, I thought it was time to intervene. I went and confiscated the two shotguns until they had cooled down.' There were no charges that came from this. Just some sensible policing from a very cool policeman.

★★★

A big thank you to the people who sent me kind messages of sympathy after my dog Mert died. I even had a framed photo of Mert and I sent to me. It's the best one I have of Mert and I didn't think I looked too bad either.

8 October 2016

When my wife's car died a few months ago, I put some money towards changing it. Cars can die for lots of reasons and this car died because it was only worth £200 and needed £1,000 spending on it. One of my grandsons faces a similar problem with his car. It's not worth spending much on his replacement as it will surely end up parked on top of a hedge in the fullness of time. My wife was so grateful for the help I gave her that she said the 'help' would replace her birthday present. She is still very pleased with her car but when her birthday arrived I thought I would go an extra mile so I ordered some oil for her Rayburn, which has been standing idle since May. I suspect she is surprised and pleased. I didn't buy her a birthday card though.

★★★

I love dogs, as you already know. But I'm not that keen on dogs in pubs. I never took Mert to the pub. He would have cleared it out in just a few minutes. I must admit that I once gave serious thought to taking a stag turkey to the pub, but I abandoned the thought because, like Mert, the turkey would have cleared the pub in no time, but unlike Mert, I would have been in some danger as well. To continue the theme of dogs being like their owners, there are dogs I definitely don't like and usually I'm not too bothered about their owners either. One of the troubles is that the owners invariably position their dogs, centre stage as it were, hoping it will be the centre of conversation. They want people to ask stupid questions like, 'How old is he?' when the real question should be, 'Why do you feel the need to bring your dog in here?'

There are still a few holidaymakers about, they often have a dog and there were three dogs in there last Thursday night and they started barking at each other, you could hardly hear yourself gossip. One of the dogs that had laid itself out across the floor, was suffering from the most disgusting flatulence, and the owner thought it was quite funny. Most dogs go onto full alert at the rustle of a packet of pork scratchings. We, simple farmers that we are, have discovered that your average dog loves scratchings but that your average dogs do not necessarily like each other. We have found that a pork scratching tossed carefully onto the floor, halfway between two doggy factions can see owners pulled off high bar stools or better still, in the middle of a dog fight.

★★★

This is how it works. Two or so months ago we had a heifer, close to calving with her first calf, that failed the annual TB test. She was sent off for slaughter. You then have to test the whole herd every 60 days and you are not considered to be clear again until you have had two clear consecutive 60-day tests. During this period you are not allowed to sell cattle unless they go for direct slaughter – another farmer can't buy them. For us the big issue is the calves we would normally sell but can't until the all-clear, we obviously haven't sold a calf for two months now and we've got calves everywhere. After the heifer failed, a vet called to advise us how to proceed and he said quite clearly that they were able to identify the strain of TB that had affected the heifer and that they were over 90% sure that she had been affected by wildlife. Professional people never go all the way to 100% so what he was saying was, he was as sure as sure.

Last Friday we had our first 60-day test. All our dry cows and big heifers are two miles away out on grass so we have to bring them all home because that is where the handling facilities are. They are not best pleased about having their lives disrupted. We can only get four at a time in our trailer and there's over 30 to move and it takes all day, it's a big job. It's not such a big job taking them back because a further 14 failed so they had to stay at home waiting to be slaughtered. Some are close to calving, some were just over 12 months old.

There's plenty of farmers had bigger breakdowns and although you sympathise you don't really know what it feels like until it happens to you. How do I feel? I feel angry that politicians listen to vocal minorities (who rarely own any cattle), and that they have let the issue get so out of hand. TB is a disease of overcrowding and poor living conditions, regardless of species (that's what you get in human ghettos and what you get in badger setts when there's twice as many badgers as there used to be). I feel frustrated that there is absolutely nothing I can do to prevent more cattle getting

TB between now and the next 60-day test. We've only bought in one animal (a bull) over the last seven years and our cattle don't have any contact with neighbours' cattle. So how else do they come into contact with TB? And I'm fearful. I'm not sure that we as a family can survive the combination of low milk prices and a prolonged TB problem.

15 OCTOBER 2016

Very slowly, but also very surely, I am coming around to the idea that I need another dog. With cars and dogs, I have in the past done some very impulsive things. But, because I'm going through this process slowly, I've given some consideration to what sort of dog I need. My son who farms with me has a working dog, a collie, of a sort. She fetches the cows OK but she won't ride in a truck so she's never there to help with stock all day long and gets in a terrible mess. She's lying on our kitchen floor now and I know that when she gets up there will be a clear mark of where she has been lying on the kitchen floor, as if someone has made a stencil of a sleeping dog and done it in cow muck.

What I need is a dog for a companion and a pal. I need a dog that will come with me in the truck or on the tractor, but I want it to be big enough to jump in on its own. I don't want to have to lift it in and get cow muck all over my hands. I want a feisty dog, one that will growl and bark at cyclists and joggers, both of which seem to be getting more plentiful. (Growling and barking were two of Mert's characteristics.) But as the days get shorter I often sneak into the house at 4ish to watch TV so I want a dog that will enjoy wildlife documentaries and cowboy films as much as me, a dog that will sit by my side. All this seems to point in the direction of another corgi, a family favourite. But corgis fall down on one important criteria. Your corgi is a prodigious moulter, and moulting dogs are banned from our living room.

One of our greatest delights was the time when we had

three corgi bitches. They would lie asleep in front of the television in the evenings, fast asleep on their backs (as corgis do), in line abreast, in a neat little row. But boy, you should have seen the hairs on the carpet the next morning. So where do I turn?

Then I remembered that when I was a boy our neighbour had a Welsh terrier. It looks like a miniature Airedale, in case you don't know what they look like. I've told my wife that I'm thinking of getting one and first thing she asks is, 'Do they moult?' I've assured her they don't, so that's OK. (I've no idea if they do or don't.) I've found one that needs rescuing, but I haven't told her that. I'm away three days next week, not a good time to have a new dog. But when I get back…

★★★

I get invited to this 21st birthday party in a village hall. That's not something that happens to me very often these days. You have to dress to a Western theme. I'm not that keen on the dressing up bit but a Western theme is quite easy. Even I am fairly sure that I have a pair of jeans somewhere, haven't seen them for years but I find them. They are a bit loose around the waist, which is good for the ego. Somewhere I know that I also have a sort of baseball player's top, it says Notre Dame on the back, 'The fighting Irish' on the sleeve, so I wore that. Someone said to me 'What's Western about that?' I told them that I'd bought it in Vancouver, which is about as far west as you can go. I've been lucky enough to go to quite a lot of places around the world, and I've always had a little ritual. I've always had my haircut there (no idea why), and I've bought a hat there. All the hats are on nails on my bedroom wall. These include a Crocodile Dundee hat that I bought in Sydney, I went there for the 2003 rugby World Cup. (I sold my ticket for the final, couldn't bring myself to watch!) I've got a Mexican sombrero, I've got a pith helmet from South Africa but at the end of the row is the hat I need for the party, a Davy Crockett hat that I'd bought in the States. When they were younger my five grandchildren were fascinated by these hats. I've told them I wore the Davy Crockett hat at the battle of the Alamo. For a few years they believed me.

It was a really good party, most people had dressed up. There was a really attractive squaw there that I've not seen around here before. The organisers had gone to a lot of trouble with decoration, there were lots of plastic cacti about, lots of plastic helium filled horse balloons, a bucking bronco and a doughnut van. There was a Western type theme in the entrance foyer that included a bale of straw. This bale ended the evening scattered all over the dance floor. It seemed quite funny at the time, apparently it wasn't quite so funny when they had to clear it up next morning.

29 OCTOBER 2016

We had a rabbit for tea last night, wild rabbit. And very good it was too. I haven't eaten rabbit for years, not that I've got any problem with eating it, it's just that a rabbit hasn't turned up. Eating rabbit regularly was commonplace years ago. During World War II it was an important source of protein. There was a time when the countryside was full of rabbits, full to the extent that it was overrun. Whatever the crop in the field, roots, cereals or grass, there would always be a 20-30 yard margin around the outside that was grazed bare by rabbits. Not only were they an important food source, they were an important source of income too. My wife's father would put two men to catch rabbits as soon as harvest was finished and they would catch rabbits all winter and the sales would pay the rent. Those rabbits would end up in towns and cities and on people's plates.

I can remember, as a little boy, staring fascinated, at the rows of dead rabbits hanging outside the doors of the greengrocer's van. It wasn't the sight of the rabbits that fascinated me, they were a common enough sight, it was the mass of flies crawling all over the opening where their innards had been removed. But we survived.

I often think that our lives are too hygienic. There used to be a man lived alone in an isolated cottage just down our lane. His water supply came from a spring in a nearby wood. When he died the cottage was bought as a second home. The people who bought it had the water tested. The test came back, 'This water is totally unsuitable for human consumption'. The previous occupant had been drinking it for 50 years!

★★★

I've finally got myself a puppy dog. It's eight weeks old, its mother is a Jack Russell, its father is Patterdale crossed with a Norfolk terrier. It's what kindly people call a crossbred and what people of my age (who are realists) call a mongrel. And I've even got a certificate to prove it's a mongrel, just how bizarre is that? It doesn't really matter to me what its ethnic background is, I've quite taken to it, and it to me. I've called it Gomer, which is a Welsh Christian name you don't often hear these days. What I've got is about three kilos of attitude. Someone said it will be a good ratter in the long term. Last autumn I reared four black kittens that were born late on, they are always hanging about around the kitchen door. In the short term I fear for their safety.

★★★

Having a new puppy in the house has been a bit of a shock to the system. We haven't had a puppy for several years and you tend to forget some of the downsides. By far the biggest downside is the potty training. Gomer, the puppy, lives in the kitchen. As an aid to becoming clean in the house, the kitchen door is left permanently open. The first signs were good ones. Right from the start he went out through the door to do his number 2's. Trouble was he only went just through the door in order to make a deposit. Visitors tended to step in it, and then walk it around the kitchen. Of course this was my fault. It was decided, on the way back from fetching him that he wouldn't be allowed into our living room until he was house-trained. This resolution lasted about an hour.

With the benefit of hindsight this puppy should have been called 'Destruction'. He bites everything he sees. He is on his early morning rampages now, his teeth are as sharp as needles, and as he hurtles past under the kitchen table, he gives my feet a sharp nip. I try to ignore him whilst I do my early morning writing but today he is busy emptying the kitchen. Outside the door, out on the yard, there is a coat, a towel, a boot, a pair of teenage boxer shorts and a mat. It's not all downsides though, when he gets into the living room and he is destroying everything he can get hold of, from behind a newspaper I have heard discussions about whether it would be wise to have a Christmas tree this year. The Christmas tree is due to go up any time soon and if it is delayed or even cancelled, I can forgive the puppy all other misdemeanours.

5 NOVEMBER 2016

The harvest festival has been and gone but times have changed so much since the traditional order of things. Truth be told, I'm not sure harvest ever finishes. The maize harvest is later than the cereal harvest and though there is not so much maize grown around here as there was ten years ago (the reason for that is because a field of maize attracts badgers), there is usually some maize still to harvest around here in November. There is a lot of fodder beet grown locally and that particular harvest can go on until after Christmas. Because it was such a wet winter last year, we still had fodder beet to harvest in the spring! Maize and fodder beet have one thing in common. Quite a proportion of it ends up in what they call digesters and are used to produce electricity. I've been saying for some years that if there was more money to be made putting fodder crops into producing power than there was to be made in putting fodder into animals, then that was where the fodder would go. Anything that you can feed to an animal, can also be fed to a digester. Barley is worth around £100 a ton. A consultant friend tells me his clients need £124 a ton to break even. What's the point of doing something that breaks even? No point at all. Politicians will tell you that you can't buck the market. The power market will dictate where this fodder increasingly ends up. It will have repercussions for food production, don't say I didn't warn you.

★★★

Oh the joys of being a farmer. We had an area of concrete to repair on the yard of the buildings we rent. We should have done it last year but you know how it is, and we never got round to it. And the hole had got bigger over the last winter, as it would. It wasn't big enough to order a load of ready-mixed concrete, which is so expensive. (If you put a new shed up, which is a bit of a day dream at present, the concrete floor will cost more than the shed.) We borrowed a tractor with a concrete mixer attached and mixed it all ourselves. It took two men five hours to do it tidy. When they left they secured all the gates into the yard. About four hours later I went up to see what sort of job they had made. The gates were now open and 17 cattle were in the yard, most of them standing in the wet concrete. We've got to do it all again. Sometimes ramblers take a short cut through the yard. Thank you very much.

★★★

It's very easy to forget just how disruptive a new puppy can be to the smooth running of a household. I used to think that I was alpha male in this house. Not anymore I'm not! His toilet habits started off as quite promising but they've gone downhill. Whilst I've been writing this morning, he's been out on the lawn for an hour lying in the sun. He's just scampered back into the kitchen, deposited a No2 on the floor and scampered back out again. He's banned from the living room but sometimes, when I go to answer the phone, he's too quick for me. The only way I can get him back out is by bribing him with a chocolate digestive biscuit.

We had terriers when the children were small. When my son was about 7ish he would bring friends home from school and they would go off seeking adventure. If they had a terrier with them I always knew that they would get up to more mischief. It was a clear case of the terrier being in charge and he would lead them on. We had a terrier bitch once and bred a couple of litters from her. The father of these pups would come to stay with us for a few days at the appropriate time. I remember his name was Tidy though it was never explained why he was called that. Tidy loved watching TV. He was particularly keen on horse racing and Westerns. He liked to follow the horse across the screen and when he ran out of screen, he would bound around the room barking, wondering where the horses had gone. Our dog Gomer is showing an interest in television as well. His favourite programme is the one about Battersea Dogs Home, and if he doesn't improve his toilet habits soon, that's where he will end up.

12 NOVEMBER 2016

When your herd is closed down with TB you can only send cattle for slaughter or to a few farms that are licensed to buy them. We had some British Blue bull calves that would have been worth over £300 apiece at three weeks old if we were not down with TB. We are full up with calves and a lot of cows are due to calve before Christmas so we had to sell some to make room. Those Blue calves made £190 at four months old. It surely cost £100 to rear them. It gives you the feeling that you are going backwards, which you are.

★★★

I was at the pub one night recently and there was a preponderance of tractor drivers around the table. They were talking about the merits of various makes of transmission oils. I'm sure they use more oil and diesel in their minds in the pub than they use all week. It was pretty riveting stuff and I think you can forgive my mind from wandering off. It was either that or go to sleep. When I returned to full awareness, they were talking about catching pigs! How they got from oil to catching pigs, I've no idea unless they were discussing which was the best oil to put on a pig before you challenged someone to catch it. Catching pigs is much more interesting than makes of transmission oil and I can only apologise for not being able to bring you more information. Catching pigs is an art form in itself. It requires physical attributes. One of these is to have very straight legs. If your legs aren't straight, a discerning pig will dive straight through them.

19 NOVEMBER 2016

This is what you do when you drill a field of fodder beet. You drill most of the field up and down in nice straight rows and where you turn at the end of those rows is the area you call the headland which you drill last. When you are harvesting the beet you harvest the headland first so that when you get to do the long rows, once again you have some clear ground to turn on. We are on the first field of beet, it's a piece of 20 odd acres, it's fairly square and I'm at the corner furthest from the gate and we are harvesting the headland. The harvester collects about four tons of beet in a sort of metal basket and when the basket it full, I pull alongside and the basket is emptied into my trailer.

I'm sitting on the tractor waiting for more beet and I see a pick-up pull into the field. The driver throws some beet into his truck. He's there long enough to 'harvest' about two wheelbarrow-fuls. I recognise the truck as belonging to a neighbour and friend. He doesn't see this as theft and neither do I. If I'd happened to be near the gate, he would have asked and I would have said, yes. That's a bit how the countryside works, there is an unwritten law that you all help each other.

My guess is that he has a sick animal somewhere and he wanted to tempt it to eat something different. Animals love fodder beet because it's sweet. If he had something I wanted or needed to borrow, exactly the same rules would apply.

That afternoon the seals went on the hydraulic ram that tips the trailer. I phoned another neighbour, 'Can I borrow your new trailer?' 'Of course you can.' We were harvesting again in 30 minutes.

All this reminded me of the first time I grew maize, many years ago. I was the first one around here to grow maize and the field I chose was alongside our main road. When the maize was nearly ready to harvest, people were stopping at the gate and going into the field to strip cobs for their own consumption. By the time we harvested the maize they had stripped and trampled an area as big as two tennis courts. Maize cobs grown for silage are nowhere near as sweet as maize grown for humans. Maize grown for humans is grown from different varieties, varieties that are much more sweet and tasty. We grew maize again on the same field the next year. Not one cob was taken.

★★★

The keeper rents two areas of land off me for the shoot. They are about an acre in size each. In them he plants a mixture that includes maize, kale, mustard millet and sorghum. It's planted to hold pheasants in strategic places on shooting days. But that isn't all it does. These areas are havens and a food source for small birds. Most of what the keeper does benefits wildlife as well as pheasants. You can't count all these small birds but I would guess there is close to a 1,000! There's tits, robins, all sorts of finches, skylarks, yellowhammers and I saw my first woodcock in there today. It's literally alive with birds. They particularly like the sorghum and you sometimes see ten birds busy feeding on one plant.

Elsewhere on the estate he has included sunflowers in the mix and the birds are busy picking the seeds out of the centre. What falls to the floor is eaten by the pheasants. This food-source will be available to the small birds all winter, this is so important during a hard spell. If it gets covered with deep snow you will find all those small birds in the woods eating the wheat around the pheasant feeders. And good luck to them. I enjoy seeing these small birds so much that I include them on my daily trips around the farm. If I pull onto the adjoining stubble, there's hundreds more on the ground. I imagine they are resting there after grazing on the seeds. I feel like shouting to them, 'Don't eat it all now, save some for when the weather gets harder.' But nature doesn't work like that, it's full of examples of species gorging themselves in times of plenty, building up their body reserves for what my biology teacher called the unfavourable season.

★★★

Puppy progress. Our house has always been cold, it's colder still now because we have to leave the kitchen door open all day, in the often in vain hope that Gomer will 'go' outside somewhere. I walk about the house a lot in bare feet. When you are walking across the kitchen and your foot becomes wet, you keep on going and just hope that the washing machine is still leaking. The best puppy story I've heard lately is of a family I know that had a new pup last December. On Christmas morning an excited little girl went in to her parents' bedroom. Her mother said, 'Has Father Christmas been?' 'Yes,' said the little girl, 'but one of his reindeer has pooed on the stairs.'

26 NOVEMBER 2016

I wish one of you would explain this to me. I can usually see both sides of an argument. This sometimes has its advantages, if you are trying to reach an agreement on something, if you can work out where the other person is coming from you have a better chance of brokering a deal. People tell me that I am a very reasonable and fair person but I am at a loss with this. Hare coursers have decimated the hare population for miles around. They are beyond the law and the law doesn't really want to know. A friend of mine raised the issue with a policeman and was told that if all the hares were shot, there wouldn't be a problem, and moreover it would save the police a lot of hassle and paper work. If someone was out after badgers, the area would be swarming with police, I would be surprised if the police helicopter and the armed response unit would not be involved. What I need explaining is: why are some species favoured over others? Why is a badger more important that a hare? Your badger is, truth be told, a nasty piece of work. Just because it looks like a panda is irrelevant. It is aggressive, eats the eggs and young of ground-nesting birds and devours any passing hedgehogs. It is over 90% responsible for giving my cattle TB (and thousands of others) and that's what the vets told me, I haven't made that up. Your hare is the most inoffensive of animals, its presence is a joy to behold. It eats my crops and grass but that's not an issue for me. Perhaps someone will talk me through it.

★★★

A mile away from our house, across the fields, is a stately home, it's a bit farther by road because there's a lake in the way amongst the fields. It's just been announced that next summer they are to have an outdoor concert there starring someone who is a household name, but who I will not name. As soon as the concert was announced we started getting B&B enquiries about accommodation for the concert. But those who asked all had the same question. 'If I sit in your garden will I be able to hear him sing?' This question begs two questions of its own. Firstly, what sort of avid fan is prepared to be content to listen to their idol a mile away rather than buy a ticket? Secondly, how on earth do I know if they'll be able to hear him, I don't know how loud he sings, I don't know which way the stage will be facing, and I don't know which way the wind will be blowing, or if it will be raining. I've made the same reply to the question, 'Will I be able to hear him sing?' 'I hope not.' Apparently this is the wrong answer.

3 DECEMBER 2016

I recently met a dairy farmer who was telling me that over recent years he had expanded his herd and put up a lot of new buildings to house them. He had taken the enterprise to well over 1,000 cows, the cows lived in the best buildings he could find. Their comfort and welfare was second to none. They were milked three times a day and were housed all the year round. He didn't have over 1,000 cows now because he had had to sell 300. He was in a milk contract that had only paid him 16 pence per litre of milk, he couldn't get out of that contract, and he had been milking those cows at such a loss that he had had to sell 300, just to pay his bills.

Now there may be those amongst you that say, 'Serves him right'. I don't think that cows should be kept like that in huge herds, and I certainly think that cows should be allowed out to grass in the summer. But if someone is milking all those cows, with all the efficiencies of scale that goes with that, and all the advantages of buying power that he would have, if someone as big as that is having a hard time, what do you think it's like for the rest of us?

What is really annoying is that milk is starting to get short, as it would when prices are below the cost of production, and all the market indicators are shooting upwards. Cream has doubled in price, butter and cheese and milk powder are all well up. Their prices have taken off like a rocket. Farm prices of milk are moving upwards, but more at the speed of a damp squib. I wonder where that extra money is all going? It's not all finding its way back to the farm. Big supermarkets are adept at sniffing out any extra money in the supply chain. I bet they have had it. They reckon they are having a hard time from discounters and they would have no problem turning to farmers for some extra money, it's what they do.

★★★

Yesterday most of my family went to Cardiff to see Wales play Japan. My son and grandson started work at 3am in order to get the morning work done before they went. They had someone coming in to do the afternoon milking. They got back at 9pm and spent an hour around the cows and chickens. Looking back they will see this as having had a day off.

★★★

A man I know has just moved into this area from a big city. He's moved into a cottage in a very rural location. He's been there several months now, the only downside thus far is that his garden is overrun with rabbits. I ask him why he doesn't shoot them. He tells me that he has shot lots of grey squirrels but that he doesn't like to shoot rabbits. I couldn't work that one out. What he wanted was someone to come with some ferrets and to net the rabbits. 'Do you know anyone with ferrets?' I didn't get where I am today without being able to put my hand on a ferret. There is no better place to find a ferret (or anything else for that matter), than the pub on a Tuesday night. I raise the issue, turns out three or four farmers will go one Sunday morning to have a bit of a clear-out. I phone the man to tell him of my success. He is well pleased and 'I'll let them keep the rabbits they catch!' I've got a feeling they are expecting a bit more than that.

10 December 2016

It's a sort of Sunday morning phenomenon. It occurs two or three times a year. It's to do with cars that have failed to negotiate a corner, or are going too fast, on their way home after a Saturday night out. It's not really the car's fault, it's probably down to the driver. But they end up in your hedge. Sometimes all you see is the hedge damage because they have managed to back out. Sometimes they have gone straight through, and, if ground conditions permit, they have driven to the gate and back out onto the road. In both of these cases you have the cost of fencing but you have no one to give the bill to. And sometimes the car is still there.

We had a car parked on a hedge last Sunday. The driver hadn't managed to get it free, probably because he'd parked it on its roof. I'm fairly pragmatic about it all, that's life, stuff happens. But there is something else that happens, that I don't understand, that intrigues me. If someone is laying a hedge (or pleaching it, depends where you live), they can partly cut through a sapling to bend it over just as long as they leave a sliver of bark intact to keep it alive. But your hedge that has suffered car damage, it might be battered and bruised but it looks intact. Yet it rarely grows after. I wonder why?

★★★

'It's the electrics.' What's the electrics? Well it's not really electrics, it's to do with computers and sensors on cars and tractors for that matter. Here's what I mean.

About ten years ago a man I knew bought a new upmarket car. I think it cost him about seventy grand even then. It had this feature, new then but relatively common now, whereby the car could park itself in the tightest of spots without touching other cars or the kerb. He demonstrated it to me, all enthusiasm. My reaction was very different, 'I bet that won't be very handy to fix if it breaks in ten years' time when someone has bought it second hand.'

Someone I know bought a similar prestige car last year, it's about 12 years old, is in immaculate condition and I would guess he paid about four grand for it. It's exactly the sort of car this farmer likes to buy. I saw it on his yard the other day, the weeds around the wheels told me that it hadn't been far lately. It's low mileage, superb in every way but it won't start. The computer or management system that runs it all, won't let it start. A new system would cost more than the car cost, and there's the dilemma.

When I was driving a lot of miles every year I had a Jag. I took it for MOT one day and the garage said they couldn't pass it because the ABS warning light was on. 'What's ABS?' I hear you ask. That's what I asked. I think it stops your wheels slipping if it's icy. The man said that most cars don't have ABS and that's fine, but if they do, the warning light mustn't be on if you want to pass the MOT. I told him that some days it was on and some days it wasn't. He said, 'Next time you get in and the light's off, bring it straight here and I'll MOT it.' That's what we did and did for the next three years.

My own car went in for brake pads the other day. No big deal but the garage phoned to say that something wasn't working on the handbrake. It's got a little plastic switch for a handbrake. It cost another £200 to put the handbrake right. It worked for two weeks. There's no talk of getting my £200 back, rather there's mention of spending another £200 to see if that will fix it. Hand brakes that work manually are just fine. I shan't spend any more on it. I don't use the handbrake a lot anyway, it's an automatic so I'll just leave it in park. I might carry a block of wood with me to put against the wheel if I have to leave it somewhere steep. But what will happen next time at its MOT? I suspect they don't pass cars without a handbrake and I suspect they don't pass blocks of wood.

I'm not really talking about car malfunctions, what I'm really talking about is waste. Thousands of cars are surely scrapped for these sort of reasons every year. Not for mechanical reasons but because the manufacturers have laden these cars with add-on electrical points of difference, points of difference that don't stand the test of time. What's green about this waste? Nothing at all. All the energy that goes into making a car for it to be scrapped for trivial reasons that are too expensive for people to remedy. Really I shouldn't be worried about this waste. We live, like it or not, in a throwaway society. When a microwave or dishwasher goes wrong, they mostly go to the tip. Cars are heading the same way. Could be that they have built-in obsolescence, and that obsolescence is a deliberate agenda on the part of the manufacturers. It seems to be such a shame. Where are farmers like me to get their cars from in the future?

17 December 2016

Our house overlooks a five acre field. It's a bit like a small park. There are a lot of nice mature trees in it. There used to be ten more trees but they died in the dry summer of 1976. I replaced them but the replacements are still relatively small. It's a long term job, planting deciduous trees. You rarely live to see the outcome of what you planted. That's why I am always full of admiration for the people who designed the parkland at great houses. They would never live long enough to see those parks mature, but their vision of what they would be like is extraordinary. Centre piece in this small field is our pond. It's really the result of what was a small quarry, there are springs coming out of the rock and some of the waste rock has contained the water into a pool. It's sort of tennis court size but it's not got a net across and white lines on it.

In the middle is a small island about the size of our kitchen table, and Canada geese nest there every year. Mallard visit it and moor hens and coots live there from time to time. But that's not good enough. My wife has always wanted swans there. Three times I have acquired swans for her. They have always come from rescue centres. They are always supposed to be free but each centre has rescued a cheque from me. Three days has been as long as any have stayed and then they have legged it. There are two large lakes a mile away and there are surely 70-80 swans on those lakes. Some of those swans are mine.

Moving on, my sister and brother live a fair way away but we always meet up for lunch just before Christmas. It's an unwritten rule that we won't buy each other Christmas presents but we do, just in case they have bought some for us. A couple of years ago my brother bought me an ex-army great coat. Great is the appropriate word. It weighs a ton and is so stiff that I think that if you took your foot off the floor, you wouldn't fall over. Not that anyone can see your feet, it's so long it comes down to the floor. I've often thought of going to the pub in it but if I put it on, I can't get into the car.

They know the swans story so this year they turned up with two plastic swans. They are very life-like, full swan size and designed to float. When the grandsons get home from college for Christmas, we will tether them on the pond and perhaps they will act as decoys and bring some real swans in. In the meantime they are positioned at the base of the Christmas tree, to scare the pup away.

★★★

I didn't realise how much I missed having a dog until I had another, if you follow me. Everyone is quite taken with his name, Gomer Jones, though with hindsight he should be called something like 'The Dark Destroyer.' Our Christmas tree went up on 1st December. I am not a big fan of the tree going up so soon, so I show complete indifference to the conversations that are taking place. The big issue this year is, how do we stop Gomer from attacking the tree? My own opinion on the matter, which I keep to myself, is: with great difficulty. A friend of mine had a terrier pup a week or two before me and he has the same dilemma, he has put a hook into an oak beam and he intends to hang his tree from that so that it is clear of the pup and the floor. That won't work here because our tree goes from floor to ceiling. I've suggested putting the tree outside the window, out in the garden. This suggestion is not considered worthy of reply.

Gomer just loves going in the truck. He stands by the door for me to lift him in, which is the only time I can catch him. I go for a ride around the fields every day and it is his highlight. He is fascinated by cock pheasants and I always stop by some so he can have a good look, and he stands on my lap with his feet on the window sill as he looks at them and his whole body is trembling. My working fleece lives on the back of a kitchen chair and he pulls it off and drags it to the door. This is puppy speak that says 'Let's go for another ride in the truck'. It's a bit concerning on two counts. Firstly, even if I didn't need to go anywhere, I always take him for a ride, and secondly, it shows he has a level of intelligence that is worrying. Those of you who are less kind may have formed the opinion that he is brighter than me, which could well be true. I dreamt about Mert the other night so he's still somewhere in my subconscious.

24 December 2016

I wouldn't mind Christmas so much if it started mid-December, but it doesn't. It starts in early November. Then there's the work. What has really annoyed me in the past is people, and there have been plenty of them, who have said to me, 'How much time will you have off over Christmas?' The answer has always been: none. I didn't envy those in offices, it just annoyed me that it had never occurred to them that livestock farms never close down for a day. I didn't get a Christmas day off for about 60 years. There's nothing unique about that, most farmers are the same.

There was always a pattern to Christmas. On Christmas Eve you would do as much as you could to lighten the workload next day. All feed would be bagged up ready, cattle that needed straw bedding would be up to their ears in straw, enough to last them two or three days. On the day itself there would be an extra early start. For years and years we were the first pick-up for the milk tanker. They are not supposed to pick up your milk before 8 o'clock but the lorry was always there at a quarter to. We always tried to be ready for him then – you upset the milk lorry driver at your peril. It was always traditional that on Christmas day the lorry came an hour earlier so that his own day would finish an hour sooner and he could return to his family. I never minded that in the least. To oblige him you needed to be off up the yard by 3.30am. I remember thinking one year that my children were fast approaching an age when they wouldn't believe in Father Christmas and that I'd never seen them open their presents. I soon remedied that, I got up a bit earlier and woke them up!

As you had had an extra early start, and you'd done all that was possible to do the day before, your morning work was finished earlier than usual. And you seemed to be hanging about all day waiting for afternoon milking. I've never fancied going out to milk after a big Christmas lunch so we have always had ours in the evening. Going up the yard at 3 o'clock-ish to milk is quite hard. You, or at least I, never went up the yard with a purposeful spring in my step. It was more a 'here we go again sort of walk'.

I remember one such occasion particularly. It was perfect Christmas day weather, it was dry (you don't want to get wet) it was mild (you don't want to get cold and you want the tractors to start), the very last thing you want is a white Christmas, and I was going quite slowly, it was a bit early but I thought I might as well make a start.

Then I thought of a very close friend of mine. He was due to have quite a big operation on Christmas Eve. It was the latest in a series of operations he had had to undergo. I remember wondering how he was and thinking, 'I bet he wishes he was well enough to milk his cows on Christmas Day.' It was a 'Road to Damascus' moment for me. I never ever minded working at Christmas again. It put some important perspective into my own life. Perhaps it's a sentiment that we all need, we should all find room in our lives to care for others. I'm not afraid to say that some of the cases we saw recently on *Children in Need* brought a few tears to my eyes. The irony is that I can't do much work on the yard anymore, but boy I wish I could.

★★★

We used to grow Christmas trees, about 3,000 a year. We have a wood and a power line runs through so we can't let trees grow too high, but it's ideal for Christmas trees. We can't get a tractor in there so they were pulled out by hand. One year they were covered in snow! That was the year the price crashed and the man who had bought them reneged on the deal. We carted them all to a Christmas tree auction 20 miles away. They couldn't sell them either. And we had to pay for a skip to take them away!

31 DECEMBER 2016

We have a field of stubble turnips that we have let for sheep keep. That means we grow the crop and someone else buys it to put sheep on there for the winter. It's our highest field, at 1,000 feet. Traditionally, by grazing sheep on root crops on these high fields, with their thin soils, you built up the land's fertility. We're trying to emulate that age-old practice and I am confident that we will see the benefits of all those sheep in our next crop on that field. The grazing of the sheep is managed by electric fence whereas years ago it was managed laboriously with wire netting and before that probably with hurdles of hazel sticks. The methods have changed with the years but the results are still the same. It's good old-fashioned husbandry, well proven over time.

Two days after the sheep go on the turnips, I get a phone call to say that they have got out. They haven't got out over the electric fence but they are on a neighbour's winter corn. This is strange because I know that the boundary fences on that field are in good order. I go to investigate. On my way I find the fresh but mangled bodies of two hares. Where the sheep have got out, the hare coursers have cut out a five yard section of the fence and you can see where they have driven their vehicles through. This isn't any old fence, it is the boundary fence between the estate where I rent land and the next-door estate.

If the coursers can drive between one estate and the other without using roads, then they are so much more difficult to catch. Their preferred time of activity seems to be the early hours of the morning, 1-5am. Meanwhile we have fences to mend. There's a lawlessness about it all.

★★★

When my friends in the pub say that they are shooting every Saturday, what they really mean is that they are going beating. That's not to say that they don't get the occasional chance to shoot, but in the main it's all about the beating. And a lot of fun they seem to have, that's apart from the trouble they seem to have getting past the pub after shooting is finished. I know people that have been there actually shooting and they have always said what a good time they have had. I'm sure that the high spirits of the beaters have a lot to do with that good time. They seem to have an informal rota about whose turn it is to carry a bottle of port with them, and it is always arranged that there are at least two bottles of port within the company. One of them is a stickler for doing things properly and always carries a piece of Stilton cheese with him in the pocket of his shooting jacket. He's had that jacket for several years now, whether it's the same piece of cheese, no one knows. On Saturday they were all having a swig out of the port bottle and he thrust his hand into his jacket pocket, 'Anyone want some Stilton?' And a big fat mouse came out with the cheese.

★★★

My new dog, Gomer, has contrived to open a door and has gone up our back stairs. I can hear him now rummaging about in the attic room above the kitchen. When it goes quiet it means he's gone up a further flight of stairs to another attic. I've tried to call him down but both flights of stairs are quite steep and he doesn't fancy coming back down them. I'm not going up there to catch him, he'll have to work it out for himself. I've not been up there for years and don't intend to. There's talk of trolls living up in the top attic.

7 JANUARY 2017

I was at the gym yesterday, I went at lunch time, it's always quieter then. I just go in my working clothes (to the obvious dismay of everyone else)! The other person was a youth of 18 or 19 or so.

He was in a matching singlet and trousers, there was a matching jacket thrown carelessly on a chair. His trainers must have cost a fortune. He had a *Peaky Blinders* haircut and a very fashionable goatee beard. He was wearing sunglasses in December, a matching sweatband around his head and he had the essential bottle of water. I'd never seen him before and there's a fair chance he hadn't seen me. I'd never seen such a get-up and he looked at me as if he hadn't seen anything like it either. He certainly looked the part of a young buck, for that was probably his intention, and in another era he would have been a fearless Apache warrior or he would be riding off to do battle at the Crusades. Anyway I am doing my circuit and he's over the other side and I can't really see him. But I can hear him OK. He's on the weights and I can hear them clanking back to rest and I can hear him grunting each time he lifts them. Boy, I think to myself, he's having a serious workout. Then he appears in view, but only on the way to replenish his water bottle.

I'm getting to the end now, I'm sitting down with my legs hooked over a bar, I've no idea what it's called, but you have to straighten your legs against the weights. Then our hero comes into view. He goes to a piece of apparatus just in front of me, once again I don't know what's it's called, but you have to pull on these handles that are connected by wires and pulleys to some weights, and like everything else, you can choose what weight you lift. He's got the handles fixed at the height of his knees and he's lifting them up to chest height. He sees that I am watching and the grunts get louder. After about 20 of those he says goodbye and is off.

I can't believe what I've seen so I go to check. There's a stack of flat metal weights there and he's only been lifting the top one. I look at the weight on the side, it's 1.25 kilos! A bag of sugar is 1.5kg! So he's been putting all that effort in to lifting a bag of sugar and a few spoonfuls. When the training instructors come in I'm still laughing. They don't see it as funny as I do, I suspect they see something similar most days.

When I was 16 (here we go), younger than him, I worked on a farm where the cow cake was delivered in 63 kilo hessian sacks. It wasn't called 63 kilos then, it was 140lbs. I had to carry those sacks on my shoulders, up some outside stone steps, to the granary on the first floor. There wasn't a hand rail to steady you, sometimes the steps were wet, and you had to carry them back down, two a day, for milking. I don't expect there are many people these days who carry sacks of that size up steps that steep. But then again there weren't many people in those days who had to go to the gym to get fit. Going to the gym has been a revelation to me. Before then, I thought posers were rugby players who played with their shirt collars turned up. There's people at the gym who change their outfits for different apparatus. There's people at the gym who take more clothes in there with them than I've got altogether.

14 January 2017

I try quite hard to see others' points of view. I can understand why people don't like culling badgers. But they don't seem to make any effort to understand where farmers views come from. I've been looking at 'badger' websites. One is sure that vaccination is the answer. 'Vaccination', it says, 'works in Wales'. I can understand why people think that this is an attractive solution. The truth is that vaccination was abandoned in Wales 12 months ago and TB cases in cattle are up 34%. They don't tell you that. I've lost 19 cattle to TB in the last year: all I want is a solution that prevents me losing any more this year.

★★★

So where did the origins of all this man-hugging that's going on, come from? There's been a lot of it about around here lately. There's been people staying around here for the New Year holiday and if there's one thing they like, it's going to the pub and if there's another thing they like, it's getting into conversation with the locals. And there's one thing the locals like, these strangers keep buying you drinks and they don't seem to want you to buy them one back. They sit there totally absorbed with the conversations they are having about sheep and tractors, sheep and tractors, and possibly the fat cattle trade last Monday. It's a whole new world to them and they love it. At the end of each evening we had to have hearty handshakes and man-hugs that made you cringe. Their last night was the worst. The man-hugs were cheek to cheek, back-slapping embraces. I've tried to imagine the circumstances in which I would give a man-hug. I'd have to be lying, injured, behind a rock in the desert. I might give a hug to my sole companion as he set out in the blistering sun to seek water and help. I suspect that Scott of the Antarctic gave Captain Oates a hug when he went out into the blizzard with the words, 'I am going outside and may be some time,' never to return. They didn't get to man-hug me! There's a table in the pub with an oak post going up through it that hopefully holds the ceiling up. They can't get at me if I sit behind that and don't stand up. I remain a man-hug and high-five free zone. And intend to keep it that way.

★★★

One of the best advances in technology for the TV viewer has got to be the facility to record programmes and to catch up on ones you have missed. It gives you the obvious ability to watch programmes that you actually *want* to watch. I get told off on a regular basis for watching too much TV late afternoon. But if it's cold, dark and wet outside, so what? I do admit to indulging myself somewhat by recording and watching films. A good film is always a good film and, like a good book, it is always worth revisiting. I enjoyed a rerun of the film *Zulu*. How old is that film now? It must be 40-odd years. Set against modern advances in technique and technology, it is still a spectacular film, especially the way all those menacing Zulu warriors appear over the horizon. I introduced my two eldest grandsons to the film when they were five and seven.

This was probably too young. The bits they watched, they watched mostly from behind the settee. I'd told them that I was in the battle of Rorke's Drift and they believed that until about the time they stopped believing in Father Christmas. I first saw *Zulu* in a proper cinema, we went with some friends when it first came out. One incident of the evening will stay with me forever. At the very height of the battle scene, when you thought all was lost, even though you knew the history said otherwise, the odds on survival were looking impossible, my friend's wife, who was sitting next to me, gave me a nudge and said, 'The bugler will be alright because he lives next door to my granny in Brecon.' And he did!

21 JANUARY 2017

As it's the start of the new year and it's a year that follows one that has been full of contentious issues, let's try to put a little perspective into just one of the issues. 10,000 badgers have been culled. Wow. You might be one of those who says, 'Wow', because you think even one badger would be too many. You might be one of those who says 'Wow', because you don't think that 10,000 is enough. I would include myself in the latter category, but then recently I've had to load 19 cattle on the lorry to the abattoir, so I'm just a bit biased. And where's the perspective? Just a few more clicks on your computer thing will tell you that in a year in the UK, 20,000 dogs are euthanised (which is another word for culled) and while we are at it 20,000 plus cats suffered the same fate. The cat figure would probably be higher, 20,000 plus was all they could catch. It puts badger cull figures in context. The dog figure is a national disgrace, it's not one that is publicised too often.

I bought my wife a corgi for a birthday present five years ago and it cost £500. The same sort of pups at the same address are now £1,000! It all doesn't make sense. 10,000 badgers, 40,000 cattle, 40,000 dogs and cats. There is a point of view that says that if you culled badgers back to pre-protection levels, you wouldn't need to cull anymore. That in turn would save most of the cattle being culled for TB. And that would just leave all those dogs and cats, and apparently no one is bothered about them.

★★★

28 JANUARY 2017

I've always been a bit of a sceptic, which has served me well as a farmer. I'm sceptical about the claims of the benefits of buying certain products, and maybe sometimes about the claims of fellow farmers. Farmers claims are not as bad as salesmen's claims because they are less likely to cost you money. Unless, that is, they are advocating a system of management that is the best way forward, which they are using themselves, which gets a blaze of publicity, but is quietly dropped in a couple of years time. Some farmers' claims are harmless. I know that if I went to the pub and told the assembled farmers that one of my cows had just had ten calves, someone would say that they once had a cow that had 11! The important thing is not to believe them. They could easily contrive a picture of a cow with 11 calves (not all hers). Before you believe them you would need to be at the birth! The first farmer I ever worked for told me to 'never believe anything you hear and only half of what you see.' It's an adage that has served me well. Where's all this leading? To be honest there's even a bit of me that is mildly climate-change sceptic. Most of the noise about the damages of climate change seem to come from the people who have an agenda, like the people who make windmills, for example. And the noisiest politicians seem to have shares in the companies that make solar panels. It's all too easy to illustrate their case by showing lumps of glacier falling into the sea or polar bears roaming the shoreline waiting for the pack ice to freeze over.

When I went to school, glaciers were moving rivers of ice and this was long before climate change. If they are still moving rivers of ice, it is fairly logical that it is remorselessly moving towards the sea, and when it gets there, chunks of it will fall into the sea. The falling into the sea can be spectacular, so why not, just to emphasise your point, make it even more spectacular by speeding up the film a bit? That's so easy to do, I'd do it myself if I were 'them'.

I remember an old friend and when he had his first television set it was a wonder to him and he would talk endlessly the next day about what he had seen. He couldn't understand the concept of editing. He would watch the highlights of a football match and couldn't understand that they had cut bits out to get it into the allotted time, he just thought that it was all just speeded up. It so happened that I used to have a brother-in-law who was a very gifted film editor who worked for most of his life for BBC Wales in Cardiff. I told him about the man's concept of speeding up things and he thought it was hilarious. It became a bit of a standing joke in the editing department. Whatever it might be they were editing, if they had a dilemma about which bit to cut out, they would often say 'Let's leave it all in, we'll just speed it up a bit.'

Likewise with the polar bears. Seasons vary, ours do, we have late springs or early winters, and just as probably, so do they. So we are treated to endless coverage of hungry polar bears waiting for the sea to freeze over. But in two weeks' time it might be OK. If there's a part of me that is cynical, there's also a part of me that's selfish, very selfish. That particular part of me wouldn't mind a bit of global warming. Most of a livestock farmer's efforts go towards conserving enough food to last his animals through the winter and to handling the manure they produce whilst they are housed. I wouldn't mind it being a few degrees warmer, with shorter winters. The dream scenario would be grass that grows all the year round.

I don't mind snow as much as cold. We have better kit on farms than we did years ago. Four-wheel drive tractors and loaders. Heavy snow can be a big inconvenience but you can move snow about, you can get on top of it. Extreme cold I don't like. Extreme cold gets everywhere and you can't do much about it. I remember five or six years ago when we were milking three times a day. My son and I went out to milk at 1pm one Boxing Day and it was minus 18 degrees! And that was the warmest part of the day! Everyone else seemed to be in the pub or asleep by the fire. There were three tractors that I had to use, they had all been used that morning and it took me an hour to get them fired up.

Thawing a milking parlour can be a nightmare. Over the years there have been occasions where milk has left the cows at body temperature and been frozen in the pipelines before it could reach the tank. This house is cold and it was cold last night. We have central heating which works well but we don't have wall insulation, we don't have a loft we can insulate and don't have double glazing (we have metal windows that let in a lot of wind), so we can't really afford to heat the whole house. We rarely put the heating on upstairs (I put it on for an hour before I go for a shower, but SHE doesn't know that). We have to run it if it's very cold to prevent the bathrooms freezing up. When I awoke this morning my little nose was like ice. You put your arm out of the duvet at your peril.

★★★

You don't need thermometers to measure the temperature, there are simpler indicators. A couple of years ago it was pronounced that dairy products were OK for you. This was after several generations of being told that they were bad. The research that told you they were bad was largely funded by the people who make spreads. I banned spreads from the house and put the family on butter. Butter doesn't spread well from the fridge. Ours doesn't spread well from the kitchen!

4 FEBRUARY 2017

Last year I had to go out of my way to see my first lamb. This year there are lambs just two fields away. Up one of our tracks there is a very tall hedge of leylandii on an adjoining property. They are an effective windbreak, so much so that our thorn hedge that sits in its shelter has some green leaves appearing. These are all indicators that spring is on the way. It was minus seven degrees here yesterday yet my son was going about his work wearing just a singlet type vest. Not sure what that indicated. Guess he's really hard.

★★★

Where I grew up, most farms were 60-80 acres, most of them milked 20 cows and didn't employ any help. If it was needed, they helped each other. In particular they helped each other at threshing time, it was just before many combines came on the scene. As the threshing drum went from farm to farm so also would go folk from farm to farm to help. When it was your turn to thresh, you could rely on a team of helpers. It was a job that needed several people, some to pitch the sheaves to the machine, and there would be corn, chaff and straw bales to handle at the other end. I worked on a slightly bigger farm that had me and an older man as employees. I was the 'boy' in all this and it was me that was sent from farm to farm to help the threshing gang.

It came to pass that one of the farms in the threshing loop was bought by a retired military gentleman. It was not a thing I was really aware of until then but it introduced me to class distinction. The retired military man was fine but he insisted on everyone called him 'Captain'. No money ever changed hands for this help but the host farm always provided food and drink for all the participants. The midday meal was usually a veritable feast. At most farms we all ate the food together, but at the Captain's it was different. It had never occurred to me and probably it hadn't occurred to anyone else there, but there were three classes of person present. There were farmers, there were smallholders (who had about 20 acres and had to have a job as well, to support themselves), and there were a few farm workers, which included me. The Captain had a dining room, a kitchen and a scullery. Farmers were fed in the dining room, smallholders and the man who owned the threshing drum were fed in the kitchen and workers were fed in the scullery. That was the order of things and that was the order in which we were fed. We all had the same food but it was served in that order.

Although there were three rooms in use, they weren't far apart, you could all see each other quite easily, and farm workers in the scullery didn't have to raise their voices that much in order to talk to farmers in the dining room. The Captain clearly didn't like this but there was nothing he could do about it. It was obviously not a term in use in those days but it really used to wind him up. In a way he deserved it, because it was within a rural community which treated everyone the same. So farm workers in the scullery could sit there waiting to be served, knives and forks at the ready, and quite easily ask of the farmers, who had been served, 'What's the beef like today?'

An example of just how ridiculous it all was came along at the next year's threshing. One of the farm workers had managed to get the tenancy of a ten acre holding and as a consequence he was moved up from the scullery to the kitchen. This was a clear example of the futility of it all and caused great merriment amongst the ten or 20 there. 'What's it like in the kitchen?' they would ask. 'Get a bit more land and you could be in the dining room.' Me? I didn't mind at all, the only downside for me was, being served last meant that others finished eating first and they were ready to go before I had finished eating. I used to get up to follow them with a mouthful of apple pie still to get down. The Captain only lasted three years as a farmer.

11 FEBRUARY 2017

I took someone to the doctors the other day. She said 'Are you coming in to wait?' No way. Was there ever a better place to pick up a cough and cold than a doctor's waiting room? If there were an outbreak of coughs, colds and 'bugs' in an area, you couldn't design a better medium for spreading the problem throughout the district than at the doctor's. Access to GPs and A&E are headline news at the moment. At the back of all our minds is the suspicion that the whole system is clogged up by a percentage of malingerers. I have great sympathy with the doctors in this. If they turned someone away, by accident, who was genuinely ill, litigation would swiftly follow. There are plenty of adverts on TV from firms who will take such a case on, mostly on 'no win, no fee' sort of offers, so there's nothing to lose. I wonder to what extent the prospect of legal action clogs up the system?

One answer could be for the GP to have a corner of the waiting room to do his work. If you had to tell the doctor what your problem was in full view of those in the waiting room, they would judge whether it merited a visit to the doctors or not. Who is going to tell the doctor he has an ache in his finger with 20 people looking on? Of course there is a downside, there always is. People would find whole the process so interesting that doctors waiting rooms would be packed out.

I'd unclog A&E departments by breathalysing everyone. I'd fine them if they were over the limit for drink driving and I'd ban them from A&E for 12 months. (I once had to go to A&E in an ambulance because I'd been drinking and fell down a steep flight of stairs so I know all about it! But that wasn't recently.) I sat in the car outside the doctors waiting for my friend for 40 minutes. I couldn't get over how many people turned up in that time. Ours is a small town, newcomers call it a village, there's probably four doctors in the partnership and some nurses yet they seem to be very busy. A lot more people went in than came out, wonder what they were doing with them? I should have been a doctor, bet it pays better than milking cows, but then so does everything.

★★★

Gomer and me, or as I was taught to write in school, Gomer and I, went in the truck to visit a friend of mine. I left him in the truck because I didn't know if I could catch him again if I let him out. Terriers have a mind of their own and are often described as 'unbiddable'. The only times that Gomer does what you want him to do is when it coincides exactly with what he was going to do anyway. I left him in the truck for about half an hour. On the driver's arm rest in my truck are lots of buttons. There's the button that adjusts the wing mirrors, there's the buttons that operate the electronic windows, there's the button that immobilises the windows, and there's a button that locks all the doors. And unlike most of the things on my truck they all work.

I bet you've guessed the next bit: when I return to the truck he's stood on the button that locks the doors. This would be OK if I hadn't left the keys in there. We spent 20 minutes trying to get the door open. And it was raining heavily. He was so delighted to see me return that I spent the time with my hand at the window and he was jumping up and down trying to lick it and I was hoping he would stand on the button. My friend was trying to feed a wire down inside the window to push the button. 'I'm afraid I might scratch your truck.' As if one more scratch would matter. Just when he got the wire near the button, Gomer would bite it and he would miss, he thought it was a great game. Eventually we got the door open, my friend was well pleased, he thought he'd done it with the wire. I didn't disillusion him, but I'm sure it was the dog jumping on the button again. I take the keys with me now.

18 FEBRUARY 2017

We go away for what they call a three day 'break' next week. We are going to Suffolk, a place I've never been before. I like going to new places. But there is a dilemma, the dog. In the past we could go away and leave the dogs to their own devices. They had access to their beds in a utility room. They were fed every day and in the daytime they roamed the yard at their will. They were always free spirits and that's how they lived their lives. Gomer is too young for that. He has to go to friends. It must be like packing a child off to boarding school, which we have never done. There's his bed, his toys, his favourite bone. He's got a collar, so I can hold him and stop him jumping out of the truck window, but I need to buy him a lead. We've never had a proper dog lead. And I bet he'll get a present brought back from Suffolk.

★★★

There's a country pub not far from here that I know quite well. It's run by the landlord with a bit of help from his mother. He's a good friend of mine. But his wife left him about 12 months ago. We won't go into that now, it's still a bit of a delicate subject, perhaps I'll tell you next year when a bit more dust has settled. Let's just say for now that I didn't blame her. Anyway he tries to keep things going as best he can. A lady from the village comes in and prepares meals for guests but she's not as good a cook as the wife was, so the dining room is less busy. He has three rooms he lets for bed and breakfast which he still does as best he can.

One night the phone behind the bar rings. It's a wet mid-week night and there's only a few diehard regulars in the bar. As is the way with regulars, they all fall silent when the phone rings. It often occurs to me that when you go into a family-run pub, the family has very little privacy. There's very little that regulars don't know about the minutiae of the family's life. They listen to phone calls, they overhear remarks between husband and wife, they probably only hear bits of what's going on, but they hear enough to put a story together. And when they have put the story together, they add some bits of their own to make it more interesting and then they spread the story far and wide. There is a name for this phenomenon, it's called gossip. Personally I like a bit of gossip, but each to his own.

Anyway back to the landlord and his phone call. It's someone confirming their B&B booking for the weekend. There's a bit of a dispute. They say they have booked in four couples and the landlord says why would he book in four couples when he only has three rooms? It is a conversation that gets a bit fraught and it comes to a sort of impasse. The potential guest says that unless he takes in the four couples they will all go elsewhere so the landlord relents and says he will take in the four couples. He puts the phone down and one of the regulars asks of him, how will he manage that? There's no waiting for the landlord to tell them what has happened. There's no pretence other than that they have been listening to every word they can hear. 'I'll make myself a bed up in the shed in the back yard.'

After he's told them that they all draw their chairs closer together and start whispering amongst themselves. They are quite happy to listen to his conversations but that doesn't mean he can listen to theirs. For his part the landlord isn't dull: he can tell the news that he will be sleeping in the shed has given them an idea and they are up to something. Their plan is that the first night he goes to sleep in the shed, a few of them will sneak back after he has settled and nail up the doors so that when he wakes in the morning he can't get out to get the guests their breakfasts.

When the said night arrives, the body language of the regulars is a real giveaway. They keep on looking at the landlord and smiling. He knows that there is something afoot and knows it's to do with him sleeping in the shed. Closing time comes and four of the regulars only go home as far as where the nearest one lives where they drink a few Scotches whilst they wait an hour. The landlord for his part washes up, clears up and prepares to go to the shed to sleep. As an afterthought he takes his shotgun with him. Shotguns have two important attributes: they can kill things and they make a lot of noise. After a while he hears shuffling footsteps in the yard. They come up to the door and they have a hammer with a glove over it and tentatively start on the first nail. Inside the door of the shed the landlord has his shotgun poised vertically, he's only about six inches away through the door from the person with the hammer and he lets off both barrels through the roof of the shed. He times the shots to coincide with the tap of the hammer.

I won't say he frightened the life out of them because, literally, that wouldn't be true. It would be true however to say that they beat a retreat in a blind panic. One of them ran right into a stack of empty beer kegs and sent them flying in all directions, some of them found their way under the feet of his fellow conspirators. They beat a frenzied retreat in total chaos. The noise of the gun and the clatter of the empty beer kegs woke up the guests and his mother. Neither party thought much of it.

25 FEBRUARY 2017

Well we've been to Suffolk for three days. And very enjoyable it was too. It's so different to anything around here. The land is mostly so flat and the rivers wander largely to the sea through vast reed beds. We particularly wanted to see some Suffolk Punch horses but like most other visitor centres, it was closed. It's a price you pay for going out of season when there's no crowds about. You can rarely have it both ways. We saw thousands of outdoor pigs, enough to supply the world with pork scratchings for a week, or so it seemed. People apparently like to see pigs kept out of doors but I'm not so sure what the pigs think, it was wet and bitterly cold and I bet they would have preferred a shed but pigs, like humans, can also rarely it have it both ways.

The dog, Gomer, went to stay with friends. They thought he would be lonely in their kitchen so they carried his basket up to their bedroom. He spent ten minutes in the basket and the other three nights in bed with them. He was a bit 'off' with me when we got back and it was 24 hours before he spoke to me properly.

★★★

This dog, Gomer, spends his life chewing things. If it isn't fixed down he carries it off and chews it. If it's fixed down he worries away at it until it becomes unfixed and then he carries it off to chew it. If he tires of chewing it, he buries it. Down the sides of cushions of armchairs is apparently a good place for burying things. The other evening I dropped my mobile phone down the side of my armchair, put my hand down after it and came out with a turkey neck! My car is parked just outside our back door. The other day I went outside. Just below the headlights are some small fog-lights. I've never used them because I've no idea how to switch them on. They are recessed into the bodywork and sit behind plastic grilles. The black plastic grille was gone and the light was hanging down on its wires. I've never been any good at parking but I thought, 'I don't remember doing that.' Then I remembered that I'd been going out one evening and down a narrow lane and I had come across a 'satnav' lorry that was stuck under a tree. Rather than trying to reverse a mile in the dark, I turned around in the narrow lane. This had necessitated multiple manoeuvres and I know that I had touched the hedge bank, front and back. 'I bet that is where the grille is now,' I thought. So I went back to the hedge to have a look, in fact I went three times but couldn't find it. (Bits of black plastic off cars always seem to cost a fortune.) I cut the dangling light off and put some tape on the wires and thought that when I had time I would go to a scrapyard to find a grille. But I didn't need to go to a scrapyard, Gomer had the grille on the lawn and was playing with it. I assumed he had removed it himself and was probably trying to remove the light as well! Don't think I'll claim on the insurance, wouldn't know exactly what to say on the claim form.

★★★

4 MARCH 2017

Last weekend, two people came up to me and said 'I saw you on Facebook yesterday.' This is news to me. I don't do social media and don't intend to. From what I hear there's a lot on there that people subsequently regret saying to such a wide audience, or it's full of the minutiae of people's lives that I can't believe other people find interesting. Who wants to know if I had to get up in the night to go to the bathroom, or stuff like that? I was intrigued as to why I was on there and eventually tracked it down. It was an article I had written that was published elsewhere. I still don't know who put it on there and the whole thing feels a bit intrusive.

★★★

Travel sickness is something most of us were afflicted with when we were young. Perhaps we can remember the apprehensive sinking feeling and the sense of foreboding when we got into a car or the misery of a long coach journey when we were at school. Most of us grew out of the problem, but I have two friends who can only travel in a car if they are driving. If they are not driving they can't go more than five miles before they are sick. I remember the first time I made a long sea crossing to Ireland to see the rugby (well, it was three hours). I was terribly sick. The sea was rough, there was a gale blowing and below decks it was overcrowded with drunken rugby fans, spilt beer and quite a bit of vomit. If you transported animals like that the ship would have been closed down by the RSPCA. I discovered that I could travel OK if I stayed up on the deck. Up there it was freezing cold and wet but it was marginally better than being sick. I had to repeat the procedure on the return journey. Which was something to look forward to!

Two years later and I was booked to go to Ireland again. I had a friend, a retired BBC high up (what he was doing around here I have no idea), who I used to meet in the pub. He was a Welsh rugby supporter and I was telling him about my ordeal the last time. He told me he had a friend who was a professor of pharmacy in London and he would see if he could help me. He phoned and said to meet him in the pub on Tuesday night. He had with him some tablets wrapped up in some white paper. 'When do you sail?' 'Friday night.' He gave me the tablets and said I was to take a half one on Thursday morning and another half Thursday night. I was to take a whole one on Friday morning and another whole one at 3 o'clock in the afternoon and half a tablet as I got on the ferry. I was to repeat the procedure as closely as I could for the return journey. I did exactly as I was told and it worked a dream. I drank and sang all the way there and all the way back.

Later the next week we met up in the pub and he obviously wanted to know how I got on. I told him that all was fine and if he gave me the name and address of his friend I was so grateful I would write and thank him. 'No need for that,' he said, 'they were only aspirins and I got them from the village shop.' That's probably the best example of mind over matter that I know of.

11 March 2017

The keeper wants a meeting. I don't usually hear from him in February. He usually goes quiet for a month after the shooting season finishes, so he must be a bit hyper this year. I know what he wants, he wants to know my cropping plans for this year and how they will affect next season's shoot. I will tell him and he will start using the 'just' word. 'When you grow that crop (usually roots or kale), you couldn't just leave a block of about two acres to hold the pheasants?' Someone asked me the other day how I get on with him. I said just fine, it's a bit like being married, whatever I do he always wants just a bit more. We meet next week, I grow crops for the shoot and if I need to distract him whilst I think, I only need to mention hares or small birds or lapwings and he's away. He loves the wildlife as much as me.

★★★

As the days lengthen, so the natural world wakes from its winter slumbers. It's a white world here today, but despite these windy flurries, we are moving towards spring. The snow covering won't last long and as soon as there is a gap in the clouds, and the sun comes out, the dressing of snow will disappear. Come signs of spring, you see a lot of rabbits about. They are busy doing what rabbits do well. They are so busy, fighting and creating yet more rabbits, that you can drive quite close to them. The dog Gomer is so excited by it all that he is lying on the dashboard, up against the windscreen, barking. But not all the rabbits are active. Now and again you see the squat form of a rabbit that doesn't move as the truck approaches. You pass close by a rabbit that is in the abject misery of the advanced stages of myxomatosis. Every four or so years, when the rabbit population starts to flourish, myxomatosis reappears to wipe most of them out. It must lie dormant somewhere and reappear as the rabbit population starts to increase. As deaths go, it looks the most horrible, painful, way to go.

★★★

I've been looking at my car just a little nervously. It's done 218,000 miles now and goes just fine, in fact everyone who goes in it says how well it goes. But there's lots of warning lights keep coming on. I'm not too worried about this. These warnings are notoriously unreliable, I drove a car for two years that told me every day that is wasn't charging and it was overheating, with no ill effect. But these warning lights can be terribly expensive to fix and should they be flashing their warnings at next MOT time I am unlikely to pass. Just so I could consider all my options, I put the car on one of these car buying websites. Big mistake: £295 is not much of a deposit should I wish to change it! I thought I might swop it before it failed its MOT and was worth nothing. Seems I left it too late.

★★★

Today we are going to watch my wife have her breakfast. She sits opposite me at the kitchen table, so we will have a good view. She goes through the same routine every morning so what we see today is typical of every day. Firstly she puts two pieces of bread in the toaster. While that is toasting itself she gets a cup of water from the tap and puts it on the table. She's been doing this water drinking thing for months now and I'm not sure what it's all about. I've been tempted to ask but have thus far have resisted. There could be implications in the answer that I've not thought of. One piece of wisdom that I will share with you is that you should never ask an important question unless you have some idea of what the answer will be. Otherwise you might get an answer you weren't expecting and you almost certainly won't like.

Anyway, we have to press on, the bread has just popped up in the toaster. She takes her toast and takes her seat at the table. The cup of water is moved closer to hand. First she spreads butter on the toast. It spreads quite easily, its milder outside today so it's therefore milder in the kitchen. As we are looking for detail in all of this, I should report that there is a lot more butter on one piece of toast than the other. Then she has a sip of water and then she applies marmalade to both pieces of toast. The piece of toast that has the most butter on it, also gets most marmalade. The piece of toast with the least butter and marmalade is then cut into two, and the more generous one is cut into about eight pieces.

Then she says, 'Where are you, Sweetie?' I can just see the tip of a black nose appear. This is the front end of the dog Gomer. He is standing on his hind legs resting against her chair. One by one the eight pieces of toast with the liberal amounts of butter and marmalade disappear in the direction of the black nose. When they are all gone, she says, 'That's all, Sweetie.'

And there's me watching all this, thinking about it. I'm mostly a quiet person, there's no doubt in my mind where I now sit in the order of things. I mostly have to get my own breakfast and have no recollection of ever being called 'Sweetie'. She then eats her own piece of toast but the black nose gets the last mouthful. Should Gomer ever come to stay with you, he likes all sorts of marmalade, but lime is his favourite.

18 March 2017

The aggression that comes with cock pheasants in the spring as they exercise their territorial rights is well chronicled. Yesterday I was going up the track in the truck and Gomer was in the back seat. Suddenly he broke out in high-pitched yelping and I could hear him moving frantically about. In fact he crashed into the back of my seat a couple of times. I didn't know what was the matter with him. My first thought was that he had somehow got his leg caught in the armrest on the door and that he was hanging there in some pain. My second thought was how much the vet would charge to put a dislocated leg back in place, although the second thought does me no credit at all. No matter, I stopped immediately and jumped out to help him. Next to my truck door was a cock pheasant in full attack mode. He had obviously been running alongside the truck and Gomer could see him out of the window. He runs about 200 yards alongside the truck every time I go up the track. Gomer knows he will be there and starts his high-pitched yelping long before we get there. Now I know what all the fuss is about, I'll ignore it next time.

★★★

I was away for the day and I called into a pub for a sandwich. It was half-term and this man came in with four children. The eldest was about ten and the youngest was about 4. The children's behaviour was exemplary. They went quietly to a settle and sat there in an orderly row. Your average child of that age would have been all over the place, running and playing. The father, who was known to the person behind the bar, had a pint pulled for him without asking. He takes a pull at his pint and turns to the children, who are sitting very quiet but obviously looking forward to their drink. 'What do you kids want?' The eldest child, a boy, who is clearly their spokesman, asks for four drinks of a well-known soft drinks brand. The barman puts four bottles on the bar but before he can open one the father asks how much they are. The barman mentions a sum that is north of £3 a bottle. 'How much? I'm not paying that much for kids drinks, give them halves of mild.' The wide-eyed children get a half of mild each put in front of them, you should have seen the grimace on their faces when they had their first taste.

25 March 2017

I think that I know my way about the countryside and the wildlife that lives there, but my knowledge is as nothing to that of a gamekeeper. Unless he knows what's going on, he can't do his job. And if he doesn't do his job well, he doesn't have his job for long. He has to be so clever and resourceful, he has to live and breathe the countryside. I'll give you two examples. I saw a fox one afternoon so I tell the keeper. 'I saw an old dog fox crossing the stubble the other day, he must cross it regularly because you can see a track across there.' 'I know, he lies up all day in the fern under the Scots firs on the top and he comes down every day between 3 and 4pm.' I'd seen him at about 3.30pm!

Second example. I used to know an old gamekeeper and we often sat by his fire with a cup of tea and a piece of cake and he used to tell me stories about his life as a gamekeeper, but one day he drifted his conversation to the war. (WWII.) There wasn't much call for gamekeepers during the war. There wasn't much shooting, well, not that sort of shooting. He had been called up and found himself in the RAF. He didn't get any old job in the RAF, he ended up as a gunner on a bomber. As scary jobs go, that's got to be right up there with the worst. He didn't say as much but I suspect he ended up as a gunner on an aircraft because he was very good at it. When it came down to it, I expect there was a similarity to shooting down a pheasant to shooting down a Messerschmitt.

One day they were shot down over Germany. I don't know how many were in the crew, two pilots, a navigator and two or three gunners, but they all parachuted out safely. It had got to be a lot worse parachuting into Germany than France for example; there was no resistance movement looking to help them. The Germans could count the empty parachutes and know exactly how many airmen to look for. All the rest of the crew were picked up the same day. Our hero, the gamekeeper, evaded capture for 14 days. He didn't go into any detail about those 14 days or how he was eventually captured. The only thing he told me was that he found a field of turnips and he used to go to these every night to eat them. He didn't just survive for 14 days in a hostile environment, he survived 14 days in a hostile environment where he was being hunted! Because he didn't give me any details of those 14 days we have to leave it to our imaginations. Even then you can't really do justice to the sort of ordeal it was. It would make a good film, or even a story!

★★★

There hasn't been much lambing talk in the pub although it is in full swing. There was plenty of talk at scanning time a few weeks ago. Most of them scan their ewes to see how many lambs they are carrying. I'm a bit wary of it, it's a bit like counting your chickens before they are hatched. But it makes good management sense, a ewe carrying three lambs needs more feed than a ewe carrying one. And if a ewe has three lambs in a pen next to a ewe having one, you can slip a lamb across so they both end up with two each. We used to call this process 'marrying'. It doesn't always work but it mostly does. One of the reasons there hasn't been much talk is because most of the lambers stay at home for a month or so whilst they are in the thick of it. Which is just as well – if you call on them in their yards they are unchanged, unshaven and largely unwashed.

★★★

I am a bit concerned that this is rapidly turning into the motoring section of *West Country Life*. Just to recap. My car is very high mileage and worth about £300, so I was sort of looking for another.

Then the tax ran out so I had no choice but to tax it again, not happy but no choice. Just when you think that things can't get any worse, they usually do, turns out the MOT ran out the same day as the tax. Not keen to spend a fortune on the MOT on a car that probably needs to go, it's parked up for a while, but not to worry, I've got my truck. My truck is perfectly legal but I don't go far in it, I mostly skulk around the lanes in it.

First outing is to the rugby on Saturday – this brings the first dilemma. All the seats except the driver's are filthy, covered with mud from the dog, so where do I put my top coat? I have no choice but to wear it. It, the truck, goes OK on its journey, it wanders about a bit but I can't remember when I last put air in the tyres.

Next day, Sunday, I look at it, and I think that I could be using this for a while, I think I'll wash it. I've had it over two years and it's not been washed and it shows. If I were a policeman and I saw it on the road I'd pull it over. I set off for the local hand car wash. I've got mixed feelings about this. I've just read an article that says the Eastern Europeans at your car wash could be slaves. It doesn't say how you can tell or what you are to do about it. Nevertheless, I have that on my mind as I pull in.

There's four of them there, they look reasonably dressed for a wet, sleety morning. I'm the first customer of the day and considering the elements, they look reasonably cheerful. They are all laughing at Gomer as he runs around inside the truck trying to bite the spray from their lances as they spray the windows. They particularly like it when he runs across the dashboard. I like it as well because when they repeatedly run their spray across the windscreen to see him do it again, the truck gets an extra soap.

1 April 2017

Slowly but surely, the lambers have been returning to the pub. And as the lambing season winds down, those that have been sleeping in caravans in isolated buildings have been drifting back home. Some of their wives are not best pleased, they have enjoyed their lambing time freedom. As one wife said to me, 'I can lie in the bed on my own and do a starfish shape, and I don't get told off.'

Just because lambing is drawing to a close does not mean that we haven't had plenty of lambing stories as they recap their trials and tribulations. A sort of post mortem if you like. Post mortem is an appropriate analogy because just as you get new life, so also, do you get death. Here on this farm we very rarely do post mortems, we usually know why an animal has died and in my experience, post mortems are quite expensive and very rarely bring an animal back to life.

The last one we did was on a very fit young cow that we were very surprised to find dead in the field one morning. She had died because she had eaten the wire that goes with a Chinese lantern. One day she was worth £2,500 of anybody's money, the next we have to pay £80 to have her taken away. Thank you very much!

There were two stories of people starting lambing before they expected, because tups (rams) from off the mountains had snuck down at night and broken in with their ewes. 'He was only there one night but he got 15 in lamb.' I quite like this story. There's a sort of social cachet to it. The rough Welsh mountain tup sneaking down to the lower, better land and having his way with the ewes down there. It isn't a tale of rape and pillage. It's more a story of nocturnal opportunism. There's a sort of 'striking a blow for the working classes' about it.

Of course there is a downside for the recipient of these unexpected lambs. Because their father is of the Welsh mountain breed, his lambs will be smaller than the lambs they had planned to have. When they come to sell them they will be perhaps five or six kilos lighter. I suspect that they will keep any ewe lambs to join their own flock. Welsh cross ewes are good hardy mothers with plenty of milk. In other industries I suspect there could be talk of compensation but people who keep livestock know well that in the fullness of time it will be their stock that will get out and get themselves into some sort of escapade so it's probably better to take this experience on the chin and keep quiet.

★★★

The dog, Gomer, is now my constant companion. It's very important, if you leave him in the truck, to take the key with you. Sometimes I forget and he always locks all the doors, I'm learning the hard way to take the key. There's only so many metal coat hangers within walking distance. Everyone who meets him is quite taken with him and should I ever tire of him I can think of five or six who would give him a home. Not that that is something ever likely to happen.

For the dog's part, he greets everyone effusively. A friend of mine was planting a new hedge on the roadside so I stopped for a chat. I wound the window down (after I'd got Gomer by the collar), and the dog went berserk with his greeting. The friend wasn't far behind the dog with making a fuss. He said several times to Gomer, 'You'd show them the silver,' I asked him what that meant. 'If you had burglars, he'd make them so welcome, he'd show them where you kept the family silver to save them looking for it.'

He likes to be close to you if he's in the house. As I write here he's asleep with his head on my feet. This is very comforting as I have a habit of going around barefoot in the house and his head is very warming. Should I forget he's there and move my feet, he will move himself from his slumbers and move my feet about until once more he has a comfortable pillow.

Last week we painted the kitchen out. Gomer really enjoyed that and was in the thick of it. Now there's something of the zebra about him but I expect that will wear off.

8 APRIL 2017

Human ailments that have become resistant to antibiotics is a big issue. The more serious the ailment, the bigger the issue. That's fairly obvious but it's a statement that we need to remind ourselves of. The finger of blame for this state of affairs is often pointed towards agriculture and although agriculture is an easy target for lots of blame, it is a huge user of antibiotics. My personal view is that if a system of animal management requires blanket, routine use of antibiotics in order to sustain it then the system of management is itself flawed.

I'll give you an example. If a milking cow is receiving treatment, the milk from that cow is thrown away. Later on, she has a period of 2-3 months when she doesn't produce milk. We call this her dry period and in theory it occurs once a year. For more years than I can remember it has been best practice to treat (routinely) the cow's udder with antibiotics at the time she went dry. The theory was that it gave the udder a bit of a 'clear out' before the cow started producing milk again. It's a bit like spring cleaning your kitchen.

But a cow's udder health is regularly monitored and today, best practice is to only give this dry cow antibiotic treatment if the cow needs it. So in just two years, on this farm, we have gone from treating the whole herd to treating just 10-15%. Spread this effect nationwide and the impact is huge.

But the issue of resistance to antibiotics is not agriculture alone. Doctors' waiting rooms are full of people seeking antibiotics for coughs and colds, aches and pains. The easy fix for the doctor is to prescribe the drugs and send them on their way. They will probably be back next week for some more and the same solution probably applies. Doctors maybe deny this but it's only human nature and I bet it goes on. Just visit your GP surgery on a Monday morning and make your own judgement of who is really ill and who needs a couple of days by the fire and a good cowboy film!

Now I discover that you can get antibiotics on the internet so you don't need to go to the doctor at all, you can do your own diagnosis and treatment. All of these factors contribute to the problem of resistance with antibiotics and they all need addressing. If you ask me, the internet has a lot to answer for. A lot of life's issues can be likened to the movement of a pendulum and this particular pendulum has moved much too far into an area that has no standards at all. There's no need to instigate a huge volume of legislation, just tell these various websites that if they carry child porn, terrorism, abuse, drug or antibiotics trade, they will be closed down. Of course you will get a succession of people in the media who say that this would be an erosion of our civil rights, but just look at where their way of doing things has got us. The only place you should be able to get antibiotics is from a vet or a doctor.

★★★

I've had satnav for years now. I don't use it a lot. I still think it's a good thing to look at a map to see where you are going. Satnavs come into their own on the last few miles of a journey to a new destination. They are particularly adept at putting you in the right lane at a roundabout or junction in a strange town where other road users invariably want to fight you should you seek to change lane at the last minute. Mine is a portable satnav. It's designed to fix to your windscreen with a suction cup. I forgot it was still on the screen one night in Cardiff at the rugby. I returned to the car to find it gone, the driver's door window smashed and a big rock sitting on my seat. I've still got the rock. I drove home with a bin bag over the window, can't see much through a bin bag.

I was told that a thief can see the suction marks of a satnav on a windscreen so he will break in anyway because he knows there's one in there. I bought a new satnav and one of these weighted pads that will sit firmly on your dashboard. The car had to go to have some bodywork done three months ago so I took it all out. Now I can't find it. I put it in one of my safe places. When it comes to getting lost, you can't get more lost than when you've lost the satnav.

★★★

Today we turn our attention to the large jar of pickled eggs that sits on the bar at the pub. It's been there for two or three weeks now. The eggs themselves don't look very appetising but two thirds of them have gone, so somebody must be eating them. They are, so rumour has it, double yolk eggs. I'm not sure if this is a plus or a minus. It is customary to eat them by dropping one into an opened packet of crisps. They are reputed to be 80 pence each, which seem plenty of money for one hard-boiled egg sitting in some murky vinegar. As the eggs get lower down the jar, they become more elusive. The ladies that work behind the bar patiently try to catch one with a spoon. The barmen make a half-hearted attempt to catch one with a spoon, invariably give up, and plunge an arm down into the jar. I'm not sure if this is pickled egg best practice, it's more reminiscent of someone trying to catch a goldfish you've won at the fair.

Twenty or so years ago, pickled eggs were a big thing down at the rugby club. All sorts of manly competitions were devised with pickled eggs. One night I saw a man eat over twenty in ten minutes. We didn't see him again for three days. This was a surprise, we didn't expect see him at all.

15 APRIL 2017

As I write here today, I am prepared to concede that there may be something in this global warming after all. Thus far we have not had much real wintry weather. And this is the second consecutive winter the same. I know full well that I'm tempting providence by saying that. There's still plenty of chance of some winter around here in April. In the past we've often had heavy falls of snow in April. It even has a name, this late snow, it's called Lamb Snow. A sudden fall of late snow can wreak havoc with young lambs that have been turned out to grass.

We have a May fair around here and I can remember lots of times when my children were young enough to want to go, standing there in cold wet rain, hoping that they would soon want to go home, and the hills all around would be white over with snow.

I told you recently about Welsh mountain rams sneaking down at night to mate with type ewes. Years ago a friend had about 50 of these Welsh lambs visited on him. He had a large flock of ewes and most of them were turned out to grass with their lambs. There came one of these late heavy falls of snow. If you have a lot of ewes and lambs outside, it just doesn't work to bring them all back into the sheds. Lambs lose their mothers, ewes lose their lambs, some ewes will take to the wrong lamb, the permutations of what can go wrong are endless. All the farmer could do was go with his family and staff, with pockets stuffed with bottles of warm milk, and search for cold wet lambs in the bottom of hedgerows, where they had gone in search of shelter. Despite their best efforts, the losses were huge.

For the Welsh cross lambs it was a very different story, they were made of much hardier stuff. They weren't tucked into the bottom of the hedge seeking shelter. They were in a pack, out in the middle of the field, cavorting, as only young lambs can, racing up and down the field. As my friend described it at the time, 'They were kicking up so much snow as they raced up and down, it was if they were racing up and down in a blizzard.'

Although there is much to like about a benign winter, there are downsides to it. A few fields away down the road, a neighbour has a field of oilseed rape. It is just showing its first yellow flowers. This is unprecedented around here at this time of year. I know the farmer has been spraying it with what they call growth regulators to retard its growth. If we should have one of those late falls of snow it could easily snap stems off. Not just a few stems. Most of them and the crop could be a write-off.

★★★

Although our land is still too wet and sticky I can't wait to get the roller out. It's one of my favourite jobs. There are different views about the benefits of rolling but I like doing it and that's good enough for me. Besides we've grass seeds to sow and they will need a rolling. As the year moves on we find ourselves getting about the fields more often. Thus far I've only seen three hares, or I could have seen the same hare three times, there's no way of knowing. What I do know is that three years ago I would have seen 30-40. There would be no way that I could confuse the numbers because it could be the time of year when I would see them boxing and mating, and they would put those activities first on their agenda, before flight at the approach of my truck.

Hare coursers have decimated my hare population. Not only that, they bring with them lawlessness, intimidation, damage to fences, gates are left open, stock get out and they abandon their dogs in distressing circumstances, which all sums up their attitude.

When I pull the truck up alongside a solitary hare squatting in the grass I am minded of a Giles cartoon. Some of you, like me, will remember Giles cartoons, there was so much detail in them. I always used to get a Giles collection book for Christmas. The cartoon I am particularly reminded of now is of a family car pulling away from the edge of a wood laden to the brim with wild daffodils leaving a scene of devastation behind them. There's an old farmer in the foreground and he is pointing with his stick to a solitary bedraggled daffodil. The caption reads 'Hey, you missed one!' That's what I'd like to say to the hare coursers, 'You missed one.' There's only two pairs of lapwings about this far, which is disappointing. They have settled on a 15 acre piece of ryegrass, that needs rolling but it won't get it. The birds come first. If I think that they have nested I'll put trays out with water for the chicks.

22 April 2017

Well I finally get to do some rolling. It's a dry week with plenty of sunshine. There's more grass on these silage fields than I thought there was and I slowly turn them and the grass into endless dark and light stripes. I bet they look good from a plane! There's pheasants everywhere, I've not seen a hare all week. A lone red kite drops in to see what's going on.

There's tractors at work everywhere, most of them are working down ground for spring-sown crops and there's much more food for birds about there. The kite makes one dive into the long grass and comes up with something. I can't see what it's caught because it's got it in amongst a handful of grass. I think it's a hen pheasant because it struggles to fly with it and only just makes it over the fence into the wood. I see quite a lot of dead crows. Other tractor drivers have reported the same. I wonder if they have had bird flu? Can't think of any other reason. In a muddy gateway lies the corpse of a polecat. It's all intact. No sign of a struggle. It hasn't been run over. Bet there's a story there. I'll ask the keeper, he'll know. If he doesn't, he'll make a story up. I could do that but his story would have more credibility.

★★★

It's become customary, around here, for anyone who goes on holiday to bring me back a stick of rock. I get through a stick a day on the tractor. Sun, an old decent tractor, an easy satisfying job and a stick of rock. What more could you want? Life rarely gets better.

★★★

Do you remember when it was commonplace for someone who had seen something remarkable, to say, 'I wish I had a camera with me.' Well we've moved on to the stage in our lives when most people have a camera with them most of the time. They have one on their phones. And that's finished off the art of exaggeration for one thing. There's a late lamber comes in the pub (it's his ewes are late lambing). He has a routine in the evenings. After he's had his tea he watches the news, reads the paper and then he goes back to the lambing shed. He spends an hour or so there, depends what's going on, then he goes to the pub. At closing time when we are all off home he goes back to the sheep. He'll get up at 2 o'clock and at five to do the same.

One night he's telling us that it's quite scary in the lambing shed at night because there's huge rats about there. 'Some of them are as big as cats.' Years ago this would have started a discussion about just how big these rats actually were. Arms and hands would be outstretched, fisherman-style, as people sought to claim just who had seen the biggest rat. There's none of that now, someone just says 'If they are that big, catch one and bring us a photo.' And that's the end of that particular conversation.

The man with the rat is clearly miffed that no one believes him. 'Right, I will.' And he does. He catches a rat next day and brings the photo (triumphantly), to the pub. Fair play, it is the biggest rat I've ever seen, it's more cat size than rat size, it's got a tail on it like a hazel stick. Our man is vindicated and I'm sitting in my corner musing that a photo settled the argument. It's just as well really, technology does have its advantages. I know the man concerned well enough to know that years ago, before he had a camera on his phone, he would have thought nothing of bringing the rat to the pub to prove his point.

29 APRIL 2017

Yesterday we drilled our spring barley and today I'm rolling it in. It's a very satisfying job. The field has been through its various stages of preparation, mucking, ploughing, power harrowing and drilling and this rolling is leaving the field looking nice and tidy. At about mid-morning my mobile phone rings in my pocket, it's my brother, I'd been expecting him to call. It's his birthday. Our birthdays are fairly close together and we have got into a habit of sending each other a cheque for £1 for every year. These largely cancel each other out but as I am a bit older than him I get a small gain. This year I sent him £5 more than his age and I expect he's phoning to say I got his age wrong. 'Thank you for the cheque but you got my age wrong.' I tell him that I didn't, it was quite deliberate. 'I don't work on dates anymore, they are so unreliable. Christmas day is on the same date every year but Easter is all over the place. I am a student of life and my studies tell me that you look five years older than you did 12 months ago, so I sent you £5 extra.'

He doesn't know what to make of this, he just says, 'Right' and changes the subject. He asks me what I'm doing and I tell him, very much as I've told you. I also tell him that I'm rolling in my top field-but-one and the views are spectacular. 'You must have had that land 15 years and you still enjoy being up there, that's good.' I tell him that I'm very lucky, which I am. We conclude the call and I continue with my rolling.

Half an hour later a hare crosses the field. It's nowhere near full speed but there's something slightly hurried about the way it crosses the field and it's not the sort of time of day for hares to be about crossing a ploughed field. 'I wonder what disturbed him?'

I don't have long to wait to find out. There's a public footpath crosses these fields and a single file of eight walkers comes into view. They have disturbed the hare who was probably lying up in the adjoining grass field. It might sound a bit patronising, but I like to see the footpath being used. I enjoy it up here every day and am quite happy to share it. My travels with the roller are parallel to the footpath, I've already rolled it down, in fact I gave the footpath a double rolling (it's called reinstatement) as I travel down the field; I give the walkers a cheery wave. I'm only about 30 yards away. They get a cheery wave from a cheery farmer who is enjoying his work, who has two sticks of rock on the tractor with him and is singing along to the Abba records that are on the radio. Not one of them waves back. And I thought it was farmers who were grumpy!

My work progresses slowly down the field and I get nearer and nearer to the wood. You have to have your wits about you down by the wood, it can be a bit scary. All along the edge of the wood, one about every 50 yards are cock pheasants standing like sentinels. There's one to look out for in particular. His head and wattles are bright red and he's overloaded with testosterone. When you are about 200 yards away, he puts his head down and sprints towards you. He then runs alongside the tractor all the time: he considers you to be in his territory. He runs so close to the wheels you can only see his tail feathers. Yesterday, when I was power harrowing, he disappeared under the cab and came out the other side. There may be those of you who don't know what a power harrow does. Take it from me, you wouldn't want to be run over by one. The pheasant doesn't realise he's dicing with death, he has his mind on other things.

At 1.30pm I park at the top of the field for a drink and a sandwich. 50 yards away a buzzard is eating a dead rabbit. It was a live rabbit yesterday, suffering from the advanced stages of myxomatosis. Offhand I can't think of eating anything worse than a myxy rabbit. It makes my ham sandwich seem positively delicious. I move the tractor about ten yards so that it's facing the other way. Just because the buzzard likes eating horrible rabbits doesn't mean that I have to watch it. I finish my lunch with a banana. As I drive off to continue rolling, I toss the banana skin down by the rabbit but all I do is scare the buzzard away. When I next return to that part of the field, the rabbit is gone but the banana skin is still there.

6 MAY 2017

I go to see how Stephen is getting on with the planting. Whilst sitting there waiting for him to return to the top of the field, as always I'm admiring the view when something catches my eye about a mile away. At first I only see four buzzards: they are very high up and are going around and around in a sort of swirl. Then

I see more and more. It's a bit like the pattern that vultures fly in Africa when they have discovered a carcase and they are waiting their turn at the scavenging. Or vultures, in a Western, marking the spot, over a hill, where someone has met an untimely death.

Stephen comes to the top of the field and gets off the tractor and comes across to join me. 'You seen all those buzzards?' I ask him. He hasn't noticed them. They are still very high up and flying in this round and round swirling motion, but the swirl, if that makes sense, is moving towards us. It passes right over us and we get a chance to count them. There's 42! They fly on, round and round, and disappear into the distance, I've no idea what they were doing, could it be to do with pairing up?

There's a lesson there. All sorts of people, from wildlife groups of varying size, big and small, to television commentators, never tire of telling us about bird species that are in decline. They never acknowledge that some of these declines are linked directly to the activity and proliferation of predators. In the next field to where we are, there's three pairs of lapwings nesting and countless skylarks. What chance do they have of a successful breeding season with 42 buzzards in the vicinity? I would suggest none. There's six red kites following the plough and 12 carrion crows as well. I just wish all these 'experts' would get their heads out of the sand before it's too late.

The field Stephen is ploughing was in fodder beet and I don't know if it's because of the dry April, certainly the beet harvesting won't have helped, but the field has ploughed up really rough. Normally after ploughing we go in with the power harrow but this field is full of big slabs of soil, a bit like broken concrete. It is decided to roll it to break the lumps up. My heart sinks: that means me! It takes me all day, by the which time I am battered and bruised. It's the roughest ride I've had for a long time. It's like travelling on rocks and boulders. Years ago, before tractors had power steering, the front wheels would 'kick' against these lumps and the spokes of the steering wheel would spin and try to knock your thumbs off.

Various birds drop in but they don't stay long, this is an operation of compaction, we are squeezing the clods hoping they will break up at subsequent operations. Birds like you to be stirring the soil up, so they can find worms and grubs. The field is flat at the top and then slopes down to the wood, the start of the slope creates a sort of horizon. As I turn at the top of the field I can see two little heads watching me. As I go towards them the little heads are on top of the long necks of two herons. They had been looking at me over the lip of the slope as if they had put their periscopes up. They, the herons, stay with me for the rest of the day but I don't see them getting any big edible prizes. You don't get a lot of goldfish in ploughed fields. Life can be a bitch sometimes.

★★★

How does it go? 'In the spring a young man's fancy lightly turns to thoughts of love.' That's quite true around here but the young men also think of caravans. There's a link between caravans and love, as we will see, but it's love later in the year, in July to be precise. July brings the Royal Welsh Show. At that show they have what they call 'The Young People's Village.' Young people turn up there in their thousands and it's all well organised with entertainment every night. When I used to travel around the farms in Scotland, there would be young people on farms who would come up to me and ask if I ever went to the Royal Welsh Show. 'Never miss,' I would reply. 'We are going for a week this year, we are staying in that young people's village.' It's an experience that is renowned for having a good time. Boy meets girl (that's the love bit), lots of boys and girls have a lot to drink and they all enjoy their week there.

But a prerequisite is somewhere to sleep (crash they call it) and that's why you need a caravan. The young lads in the pub are searching on their phones for a suitable caravan. It doesn't have to be very posh. In fact I suspect it will be left at the show when they've finished with it! They find a caravan about 30 miles away for £50. They go to fetch it. It looks OK but they find that the inside has been completely stripped. There's no beds, no cupboards, no seats, no nothing. This is not seen as a problem, all they need is a floor to throw a sleeping bag on. Now I don't know much about caravans. To be honest I don't know anything about caravans. But it seems to me that the internal fixtures and fittings would have an important role in holding it all together. A bit like a skeleton in an animal. If you took the skeleton out, it would be, well, floppy. This caravan made it two thirds of the way home, by which time it was about three feet high. The walls had collapsed and were dragging on the road.

13 MAY 2017

It started off as a sensible conversation about pheasants. We get a lot of pheasants on the road around here at this time of year, cocks on patrol guarding their harem of hens that stagger off their nests in a sort of stupor. The conversation was about the unpredictability of these birds if you came on them in your car and how much damage you could do to your vehicle if you hit one. New headlights or wing mirrors can be very expensive so the best tactic is to pick your way slowly past them.

There's an irony here. We all know whose pheasants they are but should they damage your car no one wants to know. If on the other hand, you were to go and shoot or try to catch them, the owners would soon appear. The consensus is that pheasants are best avoided in the circumstances, then someone says, 'You don't want to run over a badger either.' 'Badgers are best avoided as well.'

Very solid is your badger. I've got a badger story to tell so I tell it. I used to have a role in the dairy industry that used to take me all over the country to countless meetings with dairy farmers. Although the meetings might finish at 10.30 or 11 at night I would always drive home if it was within 150 miles. One night, in the early hours, I was overtaking a lorry on a dual carriageway, I was doing over 70, OK so I was doing 90, and a big badger popped out of the central reservation, right under my front wheel. It was like hitting a heavy log. I had a job to hold the car steady, my main concern was the lorry alongside me. I survived that, as you can tell, but the damage to my car was extensive although I could drive it home. I thought it was a story that illustrated the point well.

But then we get a show stopper. 'Running over a badger is not as bad as running over a Shetland pony.' There's silence in the group. Various jaws drop, including mine. Where did that come from? We all wait for further information. Here it comes. 'A friend of mine ran into Sid Jones' Shetland pony one night and wrote his truck off.' There's more to come. 'Luckily he didn't run into Sid Jones or he would have been killed.' (Sid Jones was of goodly proportions.) Never mind pheasants or badgers, it's Shetland ponies you need to look out for. I saw two in a field the other day, shan't drive that way again.

★★★

Rugby has always been an important part of my life. Most Saturday afternoons have seen me down at my local club where I have been associated for over 50 years. It's been a good year, we've won our league, scoring over 1,000 points and winning promotion. You've got to enjoy the good days in sport because the bad days will soon turn up. The season has sort of fizzled to an end now. I say fizzled because I had to go and watch my two grandsons on Saturday afternoon play in a friendly. I've never been a big fan of this sort of rugby. There is no such thing as friendly rugby, you can usually find some niggle if you know where to look for it, and besides you are just as likely to get injured in this sort of scrappy game as more serious stuff. I went home halfway through the second half – even the dog thought it was rubbish.

When I played, it was before leagues, and we always finished the season by entering a cup competition. The games were played in the light evenings about 50 miles away so it was always difficult to get a good team there. We went one year and we were due to play the host club. When we got there they told us the ref had cried off but, not to worry, as one of their committee had offered to ref it. Our hearts sank because they were renowned for their abrasive style anyway. That night we had drafted in a particularly talented schoolboy to play at number 10. They targeted him all night: he had early tackles before he had the ball, and he had innumerable very late tackles. Inevitably we lost, the only consolation, we didn't have to go back the following week to play in the next round. We met in the pub the next night and the young player, who was still battered and bruised, told us he had had to go to the doctors that morning because he was passing blood in his urine. 'What did the doctor say?' someone asked him. 'He told me not to drink alcohol for two weeks.' 'What are you doing here then?' I asked him. 'He didn't say when the two weeks were to start.'

20 May 2017

People have said to me that I exaggerate my reports of predation of ground nesting birds and others have said that they simply do not believe me. But confirmation of what I had heard came last night on an item on our regional TV news. Not many miles from here is a conservation area and last year there were 30 curlew nests there. One of these 'trip' cameras was put near to each nest and the subsequent pictures showed the nests being plundered by foxes and badgers.

I'll let the story be taken up by the conservation officer that was on TV. 'We had 30 curlew nests but not one chick was reared because all the eggs were destroyed by foxes and badgers, we had *seriously underestimated* the amount of predation that goes on.' People like me have been saying that for years. But the conservation officers got there in the end, and I applaud that – he was the first of his kind to acknowledge it.

This year they are erecting low-level electric fences to protect the nests and on this subject they were less forthright. Firstly they said it was a new idea they have heard of from Germany. It's hardly that. Government vets have been advising farmers to put low electric fences in to stop badgers moving amongst their cattle (though they never admit to it officially), for years. And the photographic evidence showed that it was badgers that were the main culprits. They are allowed to do something about the foxes, and they do. Anecdotal local stories tell me that they have a special dispensation to cull the badgers as well. This is kept quiet as it's well outside any TB cull area. As I keep telling you, it's all about choices. This choice is between curlews, which are in serious decline, and badgers, which are not.

★★★

I had this vision of having four hens and a cockerel roaming at will about our yard. From a hen and cockerel point of view it would be an idyllic lifestyle. Food all over the place, complete freedom according to the weather, a very active sex life. From my point of view, I would get pleasure from just seeing them about.

With luck I might find where they were laying and their eggs would be as free range as they come. And I might, just, as part of the dream package, get a ferocious cockerel who would terrorise the yard and scare unwary visitors out of their wits. And these fowl would have come from an environment where there were thousands of hens and cockerels in one shed, so I would have sort of rescued them. There's noble for you.

I get four hens and a cockerel and they are put in a shed that also houses calves. It is open-fronted so they are free to go at will but it is such a different environment to the one they are used to, the theory is that they will settle in quietly and start to roam when they settle in. Hopefully I am not completely stupid.

The shed they go into is fairly central to our yard, there's feed lorries about at night, we have a sheepdog roaming the yard all night and my son is always on the yard at 4am to fetch the cows for milking.

After the first night, all that was left of the hens were four piles of brown feathers where a fox had killed them. He had killed them in the shed. The cockerel was keeping his head down in some nettles about 100 yards away. They still hadn't finished emptying the sheds where they came from, so I got four more hens and this time I shut them in a shed near the house for three nights to get them used to their new home.

But as I said at the outset, I wanted these poultry to live free lives, I didn't want them to live shut in a shed. The shed is only ten yards away from our back door but the fox has had them all and the cockerel hasn't been seen for days. Time for a rethink.

★★★

Yesterday I had a day out rolling some ground we intend to put down to grass. I started early because another tractor had a day's work with the power harrow and he was waiting on me to get on with the rolling before he could start. On the radio someone is encouraging listeners to go to a free nature walk and he lists the species of birds they can expect to see. During my day I see all the birds he lists plus four herons and 40-50 seagulls. So I am on a sort of nature ride, even if it's a rough one.

Six years ago I had never seen a kite on this farm, today there's 27 following the two tractors. There must be some sort of festival on because during the day there's a lot of walkers go across the adjacent fields. I see about a dozen dogs running loose and roaming at will, sometimes as far as 200 yards from their owners. They are not doing me any harm and my cattle ignore them.

Over the stile they cross a 45 acre field of spring barley. I know that there are three pairs of lapwings there nesting and lots of skylarks. Sometimes I despair of people and their lack of common sense. I once heard a speech on a lay-by to a group of assembled walkers, 'We are the custodians of the flora and fauna in the countryside.' Right.

3 JUNE 2017

They have a carnival in our small town every July. It's been going on so long that it's become a tradition. I'm all in favour of traditions and keeping them alive, and you have to work at traditions to keep them going. Once they stop, it's very difficult to get them going again. They have a week of events leading up to carnival day on the Sunday. Sunday is the day they have a big decorated float procession and lots of attractions and events in a field. Every year they try to think of an event for an evening in mid-week that will get the crowds out and get them in the carnival spirit.

I thought one of the best ones they had was when they has teams of youths from each of the six pubs and they had to pull tractors with a rope for about 250 yards along the main street. There's no shortage of youths in pubs around here, neither is there a shortage of tractors, and the event served its purpose well, it created a lot of interest and it was well supported. I could be wrong but I think health and safety stopped it, can't think why, but since when did they need a reason!

Someone came up to me in the pub the other night and said, 'They are having a soapbox derby at the carnival this year, you ought to enter that.' They had to be joking! The days when I would get in a cardboard box mounted on some wheels and hurtle down a steep hill (and it is steep) are long gone. In fact, I'm not sure that I would ever have done it. If I ever had a forte it was that I had a gift for talking someone else into doing something foolhardy and dangerous!

There were many years when I would go into the local town on Saturday nights. I would collect a friend and take him in and his wife would collect us at closing time. These days I go the 1½ miles to the pub in the village (as you know) and drink two small glasses of wine and two cups of tea. I was considered a regular at the pub I went to in the town and as a regular it was incumbent on us to enter a float in the carnival procession. Judging of floats started at 12.30 and we would start preparations at 11.30 with a bare lorry.

We would start with the essentials. We would build a toilet. For this we would get a substantial bucket and build a screen around it. Then we would get one of those tables you see outside pubs that have a bench seat bolted to it and lift it on to the lorry. Then the landlord would give us two barrels of beer and some plastic glasses, and we were ready. We never won a prize in the float competition but boy, did we have some fun. It was a nuisance at the time but it was probably just as well that we had to go home to milk just before three.

My favourite memory of the carnival is of when they had a pram race. The idea was for teams of three to enter with a pram. They were to race with one in the pram and two pushing it from pub to pub (there were seven pubs in those days), and the person in the pram was to rush into each pub and drink half a pint of beer as quickly as they could before they raced off to the next pub.

My son and I and the pub landlord decided on a different approach. We hired gorilla costumes. At the start the prams were all lined up outside the pub. There was to be a *Le Mans*-type start. At the start signal the competitors had to rush across the road and race off to the first pub. The gorillas went straight past their pram and back into the pub where all three sat down and had a leisurely pint. After that we strolled off to the next pub on the list and once again all three of us went in for a pint. If the beer was particularly good we would have second.

There was a ceilidh on that evening and the carnival organisers soon cottoned on to what we were about. They made announcements about our progress between each dance. 'The three gorillas have just left the Six Bells and are heading towards The

Boars Head.' 'The three gorillas have left The Boars Head and are going back to the Six Bells.'

We eventually crossed the finish line, which was at the ceilidh, to a standing ovation. The winning team had completed the course in 12½ minutes. We took just over four hours. We had caused more amusement and raised more money than all the others put together. Later that evening I fell over and broke my collarbone. Can't remember how it happened.

10 JUNE 2017

We've reseeded four fields down to grass recently and I've been out most of the week applying the final touches with the roller. There's not many birds about. Various birds call by, buzzards and kites mostly, but they don't stop long. There's much richer pickings to be had on the many cleared silage fields that I can see in the distance, including mine. On cleared silage fields there are grubs, worms and decapitated mice to be found. The only birds that stay long here are a lone seagull, who must be some sort of social outcast (wonder what he did wrong?), and my five feral pigeons. I call them mine because they live in my barns. They roost in various barns but their preference is the barn where we store barley, should we have some for sale. These barns are supposed to be bird-proof and ours is, but there are flaws. You have to open the doors to get the barley in, and if the doors are open, the pigeons fly in as well! The only way to get them back out is by shooting them but I'm not inclined to do that. They don't really do any harm. Lorry drivers are not supposed to collect grain that's covered with feathers (or anything else) so I usually manage to keep the driver talking outside the shed whilst someone else loads the grain. When I go back to carry on with the rolling next day there's a big pile of pigeon feathers on the soil. A pigeon has met its end. After about an hour the feral pigeons turn up. I only have four now. They should have stayed in the barn.

★★★

We are in the pub, it's Saturday night. It's been a very wet week but it's dried up over the weekend and the young lads have managed to do three hours shearing in the late afternoon–early evening. They are talking all about it, loudly. You can tell that they've enjoyed their first outing this year with the shears. But as with most things in life, there is a competitive element and shearing is no different. Some sheep are easier to shear than others and the easiest to shear are usually the ones that are starting to lose wool around their necks. If they are losing wool around their necks, they invariably have no wool on their bellys and consequently take less 'opening out'. There is a bit of luck involved in which ewes you shear because you take your next sheep in the order that they are caught, but in this group of ewes there were three that had no wool on their necks. One shearer had been lucky enough to get all three and he is bragging about it. It's all light hearted banter but you can tell the others resent it.

But they don't resent it for long. One of them has a photo of a big rat on his phone and he passes it round. Pictures of large rats on Facebook are big business around here at the moment. One of them volunteers the information that the biggest rat he's ever seen crossed the road in front of his car two nights ago. This information doesn't make a big impression because you need photographic evidence to back up your stories these days. Someone volunteers the old legend that if you see one rat there are 30 more that you can't see, close at hand. I don't say anything. I've heard this story lots of times before over the years. I don't want to be pedantic but if you can't see them, how do you count them, how do you know there are 30 more? The rest of the company are less critical and nod sagely in agreement. We are not done with rats yet, will we ever be? so we discuss rat swarms. Lots of country people reckon they have witnessed the phenomenon, when, at some ratty signal, large numbers of rats will vacate where they are presently living and go, en masse, to live somewhere else. No one has seen it personally but they all believe it and I've heard it often enough to think there's some truth in it. I've seen the road at night full of migrating toads, lots of times, but I don't mention it. Everyone's seen that.

★★★

I've got these friends. They live in the village but they have sheep at various locations. And should they end up with an orphaned lamb that needs rearing on the bottle, that goes to live in the village as well. The lamb goes to live in the village before it's 24 hours old so it doesn't really know it's a sheep. It thinks it's a dog. It lives in a pen in their garden next to a pen that holds their three dogs. When dogs and lamb are not in their pens they are in the house. There's a big communal dog basket in the kitchen and all three dogs can get in it. The lamb likes sleeping in the basket as well. If the lamb gets in the basket first the dogs don't get in but stand around giving it the evil eye. If the dogs get in the basket first the lamb gets in on top of them. This also means they give him the evil eye.

Apart from his bottle, the lamb's favourite food is digestive biscuits and he has learnt to open the cupboard door where they are kept. But his very special treat, should the family have a Chinese takeaway, is prawn crackers. If they are on the table, he gets on the table as well. I strongly suspect that it won't be long before he knows the meaning of the word field.

17 June 2017

For the second time this year I have seen a partridge run over. At this time of year, partridge travel in pairs, for obvious reasons. They are not like pheasants. Cock pheasants do their best to acquire a harem. The bigger the harem the better. Partridge, from my observations anyway, seem to form one-to-one relationships. There are few sadder sights than that of a dead partridge lying in the road and its mate in close attendance, wondering why it's not moving, and willing it to move. It will stay there all day if the corpse is undisturbed. It's a very mournful sight. The dead partridge is usually removed by winged undertakers: carrion crows, buzzards or kites.

It is not necessary to run over partridge. We are mostly talking of narrow country lanes here. Partridge are very predictable in their reaction to a motor vehicle. They will fly away in front of you at a low-level and once they are up to speed they will pop over the nearest hedge. All you have to do to avoid them is just take your foot off the accelerator for a second and they are gone. Taking your foot off the accelerator for a second is surely no big deal, or is it? Pheasants and cars are very different. Pheasants have an element of compulsive suicide in their makeup. They are completely unpredictable, neither you nor they have any idea which way they will go to take avoiding action. It's all left to the very last minute, but should there be seconds of that minute left and you've missed them, they seem to go back again to give you another chance.

★★★

Remember that orphan lamb which thought he was a dog and which lived in the village? Well, as I predicted, he didn't last much longer in the village. Three days in fact. Then he was back in the field. As it is for humans, so it is for lambs. You can have a good deal and you can be too clever, try to make it a better deal and end up with no deal at all. There's a lesson there for all of us. The lamb's undoing was opening cupboard doors. He opened the cupboard door and the dogs emptied the cupboard.

He might be back in the field but he hasn't been abandoned. Every morning they take him a bottle of milk and every evening they take him half a packet of digestive biscuits. He is thriving, he has visibly grown in his first week. Animals don't grow if they live in adverse circumstance. That's a simple fact of life.

It's worth recording here what happens when they go to feed him. They go to the gate with the three dogs. The other sheep see the dogs and immediately run as far as they can to the other end of the field. The lamb runs with them. Then they stop and look back at the gate. The lamb recognises the humans and the dogs, leaves the flock and runs back down the field to the gate and the food. But it isn't any old run. It's more like the run you see on the endless pop videos they show at the gym. It's a sort of slow motion sort of run. Like two lovers running towards each other across a field. Like the pop videos, it has a happy ending. There's milk or biscuits waiting at the gate.

★★★

When I used to go to London quite often on the train, it was obvious that other passengers would only sit by me as a last resort. It couldn't have been a personal hygiene issue because I could see them weighing me up at some distance, well out of sniffing range. It must have been a demeanour issue but I always had a suit on, as did lots of others, and I don't think my face is that threatening. It can be, but it has to be 'wound up'.

Mind you, I have never spent much on deodorants and aftershave. I don't feel I need it. I try to keep myself showered and tidy. About ten years ago, someone bought me quite a nice aftershave for Christmas. I didn't use it a lot, that's why it's lasted so long. It's inevitable that as a farmer you pick up and carry farmyard smells but they usually cling to your working clothes and a shower and change at the end of the day probably fixes that.

I've only used this aftershave I like if I've had an adventure in the slurry pit or have been handling a bale of silage that has started to go off. Those smells will defy soap and water! I took the empty bottle to the chemists, I was in my working clothes. 'Have you got any of this?' I ask the girl behind the counter. 'Yes we have,' she says indicating a shelf behind her, 'but it's quite expensive. What you want is probably over there.' She points to a rack of deodorants and aftershaves of the sort my eldest grandsons use in copious quantities. I ask you, who would want to smell like them? I buy the expensive one. I don't like being patronized.

24 June 2017

I've got four sort of paddocks that I rent that are within the larger block of rented land. Two of them are a hectare apiece (whatever that might be), and the other two are larger. They are about 12 acres altogether. Last year they were all in stubble turnips and this year they are to go into a stewardship scheme. I will go into detail of that later. At present they are a mixture of remnants of the stubble turnips that have gone to seed, weed grasses and docks and nettles. I'm topping all that off prior to ploughing it up. A topper is a machine we use to cut off weeds like thistles, docks and nettles that are growing within a grazed pasture. Thistles, docks and nettles will take over the world, should you let them.

It's a slow job and it's so dense that I should be using a mower that is better suited to the task but I've started now. I should have cut it all a month ago but I was waiting for my new stewardship scheme to be approved. I didn't mind waiting anyway because there were two pairs of lapwings nesting there and there were several leverets hiding in the dense cover. It provided the best wildlife sanctuary around at that time in the growing season and I was quite happy to leave it for that purpose.

As I go slowly up and down the field, birds of prey are constantly dropping by to see if there is any food around. But their demeanour is very different to what you usually get. When you are ploughing or sowing crops, in the autumn, for example, birds of prey are your constant companions. The most numerous of these are kites and buzzards. Kites are spectacular flyers. They can travel the length of the field, just keeping pace with your tractor without appearing to move a muscle or a feather. They seem to play with the wind in an effortless way. I am minded to call it a languid sort of flight. I once described kites flying in this manner on a blustery day as being able to find holes in the wind.

Today the visiting kites and buzzards are flying very differently. There is an urgency to what they are about. They drop in above these relatively small patches of land, fly quickly over them looking for food and then they are away to look elsewhere. I'm only surmising but I think that the urgency in what they are doing is because they have young ones to feed somewhere. And if they have young ones to feed, so also do the species they prey on, small birds that nest in hedgerows and the like, and that is what they are looking for. I have a picture in my mind of a nest of young kites or buzzards, not too far away, clamouring for food from dawn to dusk. Hence the urgency with which the parents fly.

Moving on from that, we will give these paddocks a top dressing of cow slurry and we will plough them and sow seeds. The two patches that are a hectare apiece will be sown down to flower meadows, they sometimes call it 'bird and bee' mix. The two larger areas will go down to winter wildbird feed. I'm not taking a sort of high moral environmental position on this. I will be paid to do it. But like most farmers I have had to rely on EEC support to survive. I suspect that that support will slowly disappear now. What support is available will be targeted at schemes like mine. I quite like it, I suspect taxpayers prefer it, all the evidence I have seen supports that view. I am quite excited about the winter bird feed crop in particular. Last year I grew a cover crop for the shoot. They included some varieties within their mix that provided feed for small birds. There were hundreds upon hundreds there. The area concerned is at an exposed 900 feet but it slopes down to the woods and shelter from the prevailing wind. It looks ideal.

★★★

Now we have the best of the light evenings, those evenings in the pub are punctured by the visits of one-pint dog walkers. They are invariably encouraged to stay for a second but rarely do, dog walking is apparently done on very tight schedules. 'Go on, have another.' 'If I have another I'll be sleeping outside in the kennel with him.' I've never subscribed to that sort of regime, life is too short. Best to establish the sort of 'expect me when you see me,' position within your marriage, early on. My wife wanted to go for Sunday lunch every week with her parents, I liked to go to the pub at 12 for a drink with my vet! My favourite memory was when the vet and I were joined by his boss one Sunday who had with him a friend who had come for lunch. They had popped out for 'one', but were under strict instructions to be back by 1 o'clock. Well one thing led to another as it does and it was well past two when we went home. The boss vet called to see a cow later that week. 'Everything OK on Sunday?' 'Fine,' he said. 'We had homemade soup, lamb and mint sauce, all the veg and strawberries and cream. There it all was, all on the same plate. And we ate it and never said a word. That really irritated them.'

1 JULY 2017

The conversation at the pub moves on from rats to cats. There is a sort of logic to this progression. Who has the bravest cat? Who has the cat that will catch the most rats? At the farm where my daughter lives, they once found themselves to be catless. They needed some cats to 'tidy up' the rats. They got two cats from a local cat rescue centre. The cats lived in the farm buildings, were semi wild, were fed every day but nonetheless were nasty with it. They called them the Kray twins which was as apt a name for animals as I have ever heard. Every morning there would be a line of corpses out on a step that were testimony to the cats' overnight exploits. Mostly they killed rats and mice, the odd bird and most weeks a grey squirrel. I've always thought that it would take a bold and tenacious cat to kill a squirrel.

I introduce the exploits of the Kray twins to the conversation. I think the squirrel bit will win the conversation stakes. Big mistake. Someone used to have a cat that killed stoats, weasels and polecats! I defer to the superior story with fairly good grace. But my squirrel story hasn't fallen on completely stony ground. It triggers a memory for someone else. 'We have a granary that used to be full of squirrels after the grain. It used to drive the boss crazy. He was angry with us for always leaving the door open and he was angry with the squirrels for going in there.

'One day he said he had had enough. We hid around a corner, we watched about 15 squirrels go up the steps and he said he'd go in there with a big stick and I was to slam the door shut behind him and on no account was I to loose him out until he had killed all the squirrels. The first bit of the plan worked OK. He went into the granary and I slammed the door shut behind him. The squirrels, finding themselves trapped, all started a sort of chattering noise and attacked him. Within seconds he was banging on the door to be let out. "But you told me not to let you out until all the squirrels were dead and I can still hear them." I let him suffer a few more minutes, there were old scores to settle. I eventually opened the door and the boss went headlong down the steps with two squirrels on his head and several on his back!'

I don't like grey squirrels, I don't see the need for them. Red squirrels should be everywhere. When I was a child we used to catch grey squirrels and get a shilling for their tails. Nobody is going to divert money from the NHS to squirrel tails but the RSPB and the RSPCA could, along with the Forestry Commissions. They could establish grey squirrel 'no go' areas 25 miles from red squirrel strongholds. Young trees would flourish, more birds eggs would hatch and most important of all, the red squirrel would be able to stage a comeback. What a legacy to leave for future generations.

8 JULY 2017

Even at this time of year the most numerous of our birds, by some distance, are the pheasants. There are pheasants everywhere. The most visible of these are the cock pheasants. Most are to be found skulking about in the long grass and cereal crops living a reclusive bachelor existence. The bigger dominant cocks are around the hedgerows and the edges of the woods where their hens have their nests. All cocks are fast approaching the time when they will moult and change their feathers, including their resplendent tail feathers. Whilst this change is going on, they all keep their heads well down. Much less visible, but present nonetheless, are the hen pheasants. Most of them are sitting on eggs, but as we shall see, most of them are sitting in vain. These pheasants, both cocks and hens, are the residue left over after last season's shooting campaign.

Over the last months I have spent a lot of time about the fields on the tractor. I have witnessed at first-hand the breeding activities of these pheasants, especially the fights that took place, the establishment of harems, and the hens, first laying, and then largely disappearing to sit their eggs. Ironic, isn't it, that after all these weeks of breeding activity, I have only seen one pheasant with any chicks. I have seen her several times: she lives in a gateway on the side of a lane, and I mostly see them out on that lane. Not an ideal place to rear a family but it's worked thus far. Their biggest threat is usually from winged predators: kites, buzzards, magpies, carrion crows and the like. Perhaps, the hen pheasant, in her wisdom, thinks she has more chance for her survival of her family amongst the cars.

★★★

A friend of mine has his wife away for the week so he says to his best friend, who is single, if you come around on Saturday night I'll fire the barbeque up and we could have our tea together. Early in the week he checks the freezer and he goes to top up his supplies of barbeque food. The rest of the week turns out to be busy and he stops work quite late every evening at hay and silage. He manages to finish in reasonable time on Saturday, showers and changes and fires up the barbeque. He goes to get out the food and finds what he needs is still in the freezer and some food is out on the shelf. For the life of him he can't remember if he forgot to put the food on the shelf into the freezer or if he got it out to thaw. Undeterred, he cooks both. His friend arrives and he asks him what he wants to eat. He says he'll have a burger and two sausages please. 'You can't have both, you've got to have one or the other.' 'Why can't I have both?' 'If you die, I'll need to know which one killed you.'

15 July 2017

I've never made a secret of the fact that I quite like a bit of a sleep in the chair, most farmers do. It's a fact of life that where you have a livestock farm, in the summer, you also get flies. When you are in that wonderful state of just dropping off, there is nothing worse than a fly landing on your bare arm. I didn't think it could get any worse, but it has. The dog, Gomer, loves catching flies. We have low window sills in our living room and Gomer gets on the window sill without difficulty. We also have vases of flowers, ornaments and framed photographs on the window sill. If it's a good fly day, most of them end up on the floor. Of course this is my fault. But should I be lucky enough to get to sleep, to be fair, he will leave a neat row of dead flies near my chair. We usually use old-fashioned sticky fly papers to catch our flies. Gomer is just as effective – but noisier.

22 July 2017

The news of the week for dairy farmers has been the assertion by the head of one of the largest dairy processors that butter and cream will be in short supply by Christmas. That remains to be seen but if they are, it will be symptomatic of what commentators call 'volatility'. Volatility occurs when supply and demand get out of balance. Farm milk prices go up and down as a result. When there's too much milk, prices plummet, as we have recently seen, and they have gone well below the cost of production leading to serious losses on farms. When prices start to recover, as they are now, they take the pressure off. If there is a shortfall of milk at Christmas, the laws of supply and demand say prices should go through the roof. Farmers need an element of high prices in the cycle to redress the losses they incur in the down-turn. Somehow I don't expect dairy farmers to get the full benefit. Retail prices will go up but I suspect that farmers will get the blame and the extra money will stay with the retailers and the processors. Consumers will be ripped off and dairy farmers will be ripped off. That's how things are.

★★★

It's Saturday night in the pub and there are incomers about. Some of them have come five or six miles! We know them all but they don't visit our pub very often. They are here because our local small town, where there are six pubs, is holding its annual beer festival. The visitors usually spend Saturday nights in the pubs in the town. They are in our pub to avoid the beer festival. And who can blame them? Rumour has it that there are 11 buses in the auction car park and that each bus has brought two or three loads to the festival. They come from various larger towns up to 20-30 miles away. It's a big influx of people into a small town of about 2,000 people.

I've not been near a beer festival for years. But when I've been anywhere near, it was because I went out on Saturday nights anyway and I wasn't going to let a beer festival interfere with that. Most of the visitors to the festival in those days were real ale enthusiasts wearing big beards and big pullovers. They used to drive the pub landlords to distraction. They would work their way to the front of the queue at the bar and then spend ten minutes smacking their lips and deliberating which of the many beers on offer, they would try.

Perhaps they still come but most of the attendees come on the buses and they come to drink a lot of beer and to have a good time. Having a good time often includes having a fight with the people from another town who come on a different bus. These outbreaks of violence are best avoided, that's why there are incomers in our pub. But the phenomenon to avoid at all costs are the many hen parties that attend. The drinking and violence of women can be off the scale.

★★★

My second eldest grandson is messing about with his car; he calls it tidying up. The dog Gomer is helping him. I'm hoping to see the bonnet go up and for him to check the oil and water. This is one of life's longshots. They wouldn't even give you odds for it on those TV betting adverts. He comes into the kitchen, sprays himself liberally with an aerosol deodorant he uses so much that he kills the flies in the kitchen in the process with the clouds of spray that go everywhere, and nearly kills me, and declares that he is off now. He is off to the local swimming pool where he works as a lifesaver when he is home from college. His car is parked out in the hot sun all day.

At about 6 o'clock he drives home and is immediately aware of a vile smell in the back. What's the cause of that smell? One of his first thoughts is that he can't remember seeing Gomer when he drove off that morning. It is almost inevitable that the second thought is that perhaps the dog had somehow got into the back of the car, been there all day and succumbed to the heat.

After three more miles the smell is unbearable so he pulls up and gets out to open the back of the car. He does this with great trepidation, fearing the worst. He opens the boot and all that is in there is a pair of socks he wore for cricket on Saturday. With a sigh of relief, he throws them over the hedge and continues home.

29 July 2017

In this competitive world, being first with the news down at the pub are two events that stand out as being of great importance. They are the birth of the first lamb; and the first one to get the combine out.

Having the first lamb is often the result of a mishap, an unplanned liaison between ewe and ram or more likely one of last year's late lambs that had missed being castrated, that had got in with your ewes. It might well be that your main flock are not due to start lambing for another month yet, but nonetheless, a lamb is a lamb and you score all the points.

Being first out with the combine is much more competitive. Similar crops in the same area ripen at the same time so there's usually only a couple of days between first and last. Thus when someone comes into the pub at about 10 o'clock covered in dust and barley hairs and says that he has made a start today on the winter barley, his news is received by a tight-lipped audience. What they are saying to themselves is, 'I could have started today but the forecast is good so I thought I would start tomorrow. But I could have been first!'

Within a few days they are all combining and we hear all about it on a regular basis. What's gone right, and what's gone wrong and of high, record-breaking yields in every field.

But the next big news on the combine front is who is the first one to 'blow up' the combine. Blowing up the combine can take two forms. The drum that threshes the grain goes around at huge speed so if something mechanical should go wrong, the resulting noise can be frightening, hence the term 'blown up'. This mechanical failure is rarely the fault of the operator but he usually gets the blame in the pub and the stigma is all his.

Then there is the blowing up due to foreign bodies entering the mechanism. Foreign bodies can take various forms. Sometimes it is a piece of metal that has broken off a machine that was used in a previous operation – a few years ago it was bike that had been thrown over the hedge. The combine made the traditional blowing up noise but emerged relatively unscathed, which was more than could be said for the bike.

The most common problem with foreign bodies, especially if some of the crop is laid down on the ground, and if the operator has to lower the cutter to lift it and cut it all, is big stones. Stones can shatter within the mechanism, they make a lot of noise but you can usually live with the damage. Some stones are made of sterner stuff and go through the whole system and come out at the other end with barely a scratch. But they have wreaked havoc with the combine's innards along the way. Stone is a benign sort of name. Stones that manage to get into combines are usually called rocks, and rock is a much more sinister name. I noticed the first local combine starting work on the winter barley. When I went past two hours later, half the field was cleared but there was no sign of the combine. In the pub that night we heard that they had picked up a rock. Thus we had the first 'combine out' story and the 'blown up' story on the same day. It was good to get them both out of the way. We can get back to gossiping about people, which is much more interesting.

★★★

I've just been handed a bunch of raffle tickets to sell. I'm not good at selling raffle tickets, it's a job I hate. Years ago we used to get quite a lot of salesmen calling regularly at the farm and if we had raffle tickets to sell, we would leave them lying on the kitchen table and sell them to these callers. They had put themselves in a difficult place: how do you say no to buying a raffle ticket if you are in turn trying to sell something? We don't get many callers now so I will end up buying some tickets myself and writing family members' names on the counterfoils so that I will have some sold tickets and money to hand back.

Years ago I organised a Christmas raffle for the rugby club. It was a big raffle with about 20 prizes. I shall never do another, it was more work and more complicated than I had imagined. I eventually did the draw and made sure that there were a couple of committee members there to see that it was all done fairly. We came to the last two prizes. They were a box of chocolates and a turkey. The chocolates were won by someone who lived five miles away and turkey was won by someone who lived in Blackpool! At the time it seemed eminently sensible and common sense to swap the prizes over and take the turkey five miles and post the chocolates to Blackpool. These days it would be seen as a 'green' solution to a problem. That is what I did. But because it was a good story it got talked about and the story reached the wrong ears. Someone reported me to the body that licences raffles and they banned me from promoting another raffle! I don't know how long the ban lasts – hopefully forever.

5 AUGUST 2017

I was reading an article about pig farming the other day. It told me that there were 400,000 breeding sows in this country. This came as a complete surprise to me. My two eldest grandsons eat so much bacon and sausage for breakfast that I thought that they had surely eaten all the pigs by now. Not that I've got a problem with feeding them, the standard of catering goes up by leaps and bounds when they are about. Vegetables don't just go from saucepan to plate anymore. They go into serving bowls on the table. But you have to have your wits about you to get your share. Whatever next, a tablecloth? I don't always get the same food as them, I get the scraps. The dog gets first pick of the scraps. I come after him, but they are still good scraps.

★★★

Pig and poultry sectors don't get taxpayers' support, politicians are quick to point this out, so let's see what's happened to them. Well, the sow numbers have more than halved in the last 20 years. Pig farmers have welfare standards imposed on them, such as no sow stalls, and these high standards have made them uncompetitive. What happens then? We import the pig meat deficit from countries that still have sow stalls. Are you OK with that? I'm not. But it's been allowed to happen. Most sows in this country live and breed outside. In cold wet weather they go back into warm insulated huts. In hot weather they wallow in muddy hollows. Apart from the restrictions of electric fences, they very much do as pigs like to do.

Most of these sows are to be found living in the eastern half of the country where there is plenty of straw. Pigs like straw, they prefer it to metal bars.

What's happened to the poultry industry? The consumer demand for poultry meat continues to expand and the industry has expanded accordingly. Consumers like a nice fresh chicken or chicken portions. They particularly like chicken if it's cheap. To get cheap chicken it has to produced on an industrial scale. The irony is that people love a nice fresh chicken to put in the oven, especially if that chicken cost less than a fiver. But they prefer to ignore what sort of life that chicken has had before it got to them. You could let chickens run outside but it doesn't work as well as it does with pigs. Chickens don't like getting their feathers wet and prefer to stay indoors on wet days. You can have free range chickens but it won't be as cheap. Most eggs are free range now and people like this, it gives them comfort. But the truth is that about 70% of hens never put a foot outside the sheds, preferring to live their lives close to food, water and where they lay their eggs.

Politicians, who largely know nothing about farming, point to the New Zealand example. Support was withdrawn from New Zealand farming overnight, I think in the 1980s. It caused untold hardships and change. They have successfully come through that now. But there were some serious animal welfare issues along the way. They could only survive by cutting costs and the easiest cost to cut is staffing levels. If you have two people looking after 1,000 plus cows or one man looking after 1,200 ewes, standards of care will suffer.

It was probably the animals themselves that won the day. At staffing levels like that, only fittest animals will survive and that in turn precipitates a natural selection process. Most livestock production in the UK is based on family farms. No one owes us a living, I understand that. But in the world that is to come, what we have seen happen to pigs and poultry and in New Zealand is not necessarily what we want and neither is it the answer. This is not a threat. Just be careful what you wish for.

***

12 August 2017

Yesterday I lost one of the little screws that holds my reading/writing glasses together. I've put some fuse wire through where the screw was (remember fuse wire?). But I can't get the wire tight enough to hold the lens in, so I've got a rubber band doubled up holding the lens. The worrying thing is that although the band goes right across the middle of the lens, I can't see it. It's a small blue rubber band. I got it out of the fridge where it was holding some spring onions together. Anyway, today I am going to talk about food. My food, and my breakfast in particular. The basis of my breakfast is always two pieces of toast. On these is put some butter. I banned spreads from the house about two years ago when it was discovered that butter was actually OK for you and not the health risk we had been told for 30 years. Surprise, surprise, we had been told that butter was a health risk by none other than the people who make spreads. The worrying thing is that we believed them! I spread my butter fairly liberally as it's forecast to run out before Christmas, so best make the most of it.

It's what goes on top of these two pieces of toast that varies. For a week I might have two fried eggs and tomato ketchup. Then I tire of that and get the marmite out. But the marmite is rarely used alone. Plum jam on top of marmite is excellent. It must be to do with the mix of sweet and savoury. If you want just savoury, try chopped up spring onion on top of the marmite. Sometimes I have beans on toast, or tinned tomatoes on toast, but always with the marmite. By then it's probably time to go back to the fried eggs again.

I do not breakfast alone. The dog Gomer has his head on my knee. He's been sharing my wife's toast and marmalade for some time and now he is bent on sharing mine. Sometimes it's bits I have dropped and sometimes it's passed to him. I don't mean to drop things onto the floor but I pass him things as part of an experiment. I know you shouldn't feed pets from the table but we are where we are. I was flicking the TV channels the other day and I came across this programme about dog behaviour. This family were all sitting down together for a meal and had put the food on the table. Then they put the dog on the table. During the meal, and whilst they were eating, the dog wandered the table and picked bits of food off their plates. If the dog had difficulty picking a piece of food up, they would pick it up for him with their forks and feed him.

Back to Gomer. He is a picky eater. Sometimes he refuses to eat food we put in his bowl for him. There are certain brands of tinned dog food he refuses to eat at any cost. I have discovered, however, that he will eat anything that has been on our table. I found this out one day when I dropped a spring onion on the floor. No wonder I couldn't find it, he'd eaten it. I like spring onions but I cut some of the green off the top and the bit with the root on at the bottom. He eats all that. He will eat marmite, no matter how thick I put it on. I thought I'd beat him one day, I gave him some chilli: he ate the lot. Today I had a different sort of breakfast. I had my first feed of field mushrooms. They were too good to drop on the floor. Or put in the dog.

★★★

The old farmer and his son go into the farmhouse for a mid-morning drink. Whilst they are in the kitchen the grandson comes down the stairs. He has arrived home from college during the night, for the summer break. There are now three generations in the kitchen. Without any pre-amble the grandson tells his dad he needs some money, that he had to borrow money to see himself through until the end of term and he has to pay it back immediately. 'Borrow money!' explodes his father. 'Borrow money! I've just been looking at your car: all the tyres are bald, it's scratched and dented all round. The exhaust is falling off and the inside looks as if it has been trashed. You've not done well in your exams and I bet you've spent all your money on drink and girls. Your mother told me she sent you some money a month ago and I bet she's sent money she hasn't told me about.' He's running out of steam now and he looks to his father for support. The older man shakes his head. 'Somehow I think I've heard all this conversation before.'

29 AUGUST 2017

When my children were at primary school in the village, the headmaster suggested that I start a parent/teacher association. The other teachers, there were only three including the head, were not that keen on calling it a PTA. I remember thinking at the time that the teachers didn't want to be formally associated with some of the parents. (I wasn't that bothered myself.) Thus we called it the 'Friends of xx School.' I started it off and chaired it for ten years, until my children left. There are memories of that time. There was a swimming pool at our local town, it's still the same one, but it wasn't open to the public, it was hired by organisations who had to provide a qualified lifesaver. I was one of the lifesavers in the area so, for ten years, once a week, I would go on the bus with the children to their swimming class. I remember in the notoriously hot summer of 1976 I opened the pool five days a week throughout the summer holidays for two hours a day so that all local children could go swimming. It was hard work, there was a limit to how many could go into the pool at a time so we had this system of coloured arm bands. The trouble was that once they were in you had a job to get them back out. Milking the cows when I got home afterwards was a tranquil experience!

I've just thought of another escapade at that pool. For years I used to run the local youth club. We used to go swimming. I would arrive in the village in my car, there would be lots of children there but no other parents. It was five miles to the pool and hence there was a dilemma. If I took half of them to the pool and went back to fetch the other half, I was responsible for the first half who were at the pool unattended. It was unsatisfactory. I resolved it by taking them all in one load. Thirteen children plus me in a Morris Oxford! There were three in the boot. Two of them were mine. I dread to think what modern health and safety would think! The children thought it was great so they told their parents about it. I had phone calls of complaint but they got short shrift from me. There were three parents with cars there the next week!

One of the main functions of the 'Friends' was to raise money for extras for the school and once a year we had a dance in the village hall. I was the only man on the committee and every year we fell out over the choice of music. There was an old farmer lived up in the hills near here (he was ten years older than me.) He had set himself up as a DJ. He didn't have a very sophisticated set-up, he had one deck and one loudspeaker and no lights. He wasn't very sophisticated himself, he always wore a short-sleeved Fair Isle pullover and his teeth stuck out. He was nowhere near the young mothers' idea of cool. But he had two redeeming features. He had all the latest records and he only charged £13! That meant that as soon as the committee had paid their entrance fee, you had paid for the hall and the disco and were in profit.

Anyway, at our monthly Friends meetings I used to try to get a speaker and one month we had the village policeman. He was telling us about his career. When he finished his training he was posted to the main police station in our county town. He spent the first day at the desk. On his second day the sergeant said, 'I'll take you to do your first booking.' Our policeman asked how he could be so sure that they would find someone to 'book.' 'That's easy', says the sergeant, 'It's market day today, we'll go and get a farmer.' So they went to the main road near the market and the first three Land Rovers and trailers they stopped had minor defects and were duly 'booked'. Farmers, including me (especially including me), had a cavalier approach to lights and the like on trailers. Bulbs and lenses get broken in the rough and tumble of farm life. Twenty years ago it was only big estates and posh farmers that had lights that worked on the stuff you pulled behind tractors. Things are different now because you get points on your licence to accompany the fine. Over the years things change.

The market in our county town is at a different site. The former site is now a supermarket, as is the way with these things. Other things don't change. On market days they cordon off a lay-by and stop traffic, that's OK. But if the policeman steps out to wave a lorry in and he sees a farmer's trailer close behind, he waves the lorry on and stops the farmer. Little has changed really, since my policeman and 40 years ago. It is the very worst sort of biased stop-and-search!

26 AUGUST 2017

The recent weather patterns have alternated between warm sunshine and torrential downpours. As a result, the harvest has been progressing slowly and has been very much a case of snatching what you can, when you can. A lot of harvesting has been done in the evenings and 10 o'clock seems to be the proper time to finish for the day. There is thus the influx of harvesters into the pub at around 10.30. For people like me, who like watching people, there is much to see. For a start, they are still in their working clothes, which is fair enough, but it is the state of these clothes which tells what sort of day they have had. There will be dust, grease and oil aplenty and the more there is, the worse the day. But it's their eyes that are the giveaway.

If they have had a really bad day, their eyes have a haunted look about them. Not for them the luxury of an anonymous sidle up to the bar. There's few secrets in farming, everyone can see what you are doing. Before they can take two or three steps from the door, someone will say, 'Your combine has been stopped for three hours, what's wrong with it?' These mechanical giants slumber in a shed for nine or ten months of the year but when they are woken up for two or three months frenzied work, they break down with regularity. 'The hydraulics are playing up,' is the most common answer. If it's a new combine, so much more the merriment of the assembled throng. I often wonder why, after a long hard day, they don't go straight home. I know that when I used to do a lot of driving, I would get home in the early hours after a two or three hour drive, and I would have to watch TV for half an hour before I could get to sleep. Perhaps they need that half hour in the pub to unwind. But half an hour in the pub after a mechanical breakdown has got to be a sort of masochism. The post mortem goes on until closing time and they eventually go home with lots of advice ringing in their ears. Of sympathy, there is none.

★★★

All the cereals we had this year were 30 acres of spring barley. We cleared that about two weeks ago. We didn't allow it to fully ripen for the combine. We chopped it up, straw and grain, and made silage of it. This is best done when the grain is still soft and 'cheesy', so that the cows are able to digest it. Into the stubble that was left we have drilled a kale/rape hybrid that, with luck, will provide winter feed for the dry cows and heifers. This showery weather should suit it just fine and I go up there every day to check on its progress.

Earlier in the year we put in some small patches of root crop mixes for the shoot. These are growing well now and have attracted lapwings. Some days there's seven up there. The next day there's 16. I had assumed that there was a flock of seven and some days they joined up with a flock of nine. That's two flocks. But there could be three flocks. A seven, a nine and a 16. There's no way of telling. The people who reckon that they can count wild birds and animals have no more idea than I have, and I haven't a clue! But at least I am honest about it.

What I do know is that these are the fields that the lapwings seem to prefer and that we will see them now all winter. What I also know is that just over the fence is a six acre plot that we have sown to a wild bird winter feed mix and next to that is three acres dedicated to a lapwing-friendly environment. We have left patches in this plot for lapwings to nest in. For reasons that I don't know these are called scrapes. It's all there for them, so we just hope for the best. But with the best will in the world... Cover, feed and nesting site are all close at hand, a mere wing beat away. Trouble is, it's also only a wing beat for kites, buzzards, carrion crows, magpies, the predator list seems endless and I've not mentioned foxes and badgers and walkers' dogs.

★★★

Vintage tractors are quite a big things around here. They are mostly owned by farmers and those who work on farms. But they are also owned by people from all walks of life, usually those with a connection to the land and farming, even if that link goes back a generation or so. Vintage tractors are in great demand at this time of year: people like them to be at fêtes and the like. The man who works here has a 1950s David Brown and he took it to three fêtes last weekend. They all belong to a tractor club and they do tractor runs throughout the year that can include 50 tractors in a long procession. Attendances at fêtes and tractor runs is all done at their own expense and in the aid of charity. But there is a problem. Tractors that work on farms and spend most of their lives in fields, are allowed to use red diesel which is a lot cheaper than the 'white' diesel that is used in cars and lorries. Vintage tractor drivers, making their way to charity events, are being regularly stopped by police to check that they are using white diesel. So what's all that about? With so much wrong in the world today, does it really matter?

2 SEPTEMBER 2017

There's a bit of detail in this, but you need the detail in order to appreciate the inconvenience. We are a bit short of grass for the cows at home but have plenty two miles away. So we have been cutting this 'away' grass and have a machine that will pick up the cut grass and bring it home. The tractor driver takes this wagon to the field, takes it off, puts the mower on, cuts enough grass, puts the wagon back on, picks up the grass and brings it home. The mower is left in the field. The keeper is on his rounds at dusk one night, hears a tractor in the field and goes for a chat. He finds a strange tractor backing up to our mower to hitch up to it. The stranger on the tractor sees the keeper and makes off at high speed. We go to fetch the mower home the next day and, whilst there, a truck drives up apparently to see if the mower is still there. Now we have to go with the mower, take it home, then go with the wagon. It's an extra hour's work a day.

★★★

The two most important people in a dairy farmer's life are the bank manager and the milk tanker driver. Over the last few difficult years there has been quite a lot of contact with the bank manager but it occurred to me the other day that I haven't seen the tanker driver for over 12 months. The number of times you see the tanker driver is directly linked to the time he comes to collect the milk. Ours comes, at present, at 6-6.30 in the evening, which is the time of day we are having our evening meal or I am going into the other room to watch the news.

But his 6 o'clockish visit doesn't go unnoticed. We can hear the lorry arrive but we can't see it. The dog Gomer can hear it as well. He skips out the kitchen door when the lorry arrives and comes back about ten minutes later. He is well pleased with himself. His is licking his chops and under his jaw is a little goatee beard that is white with milk. This tells me two things. One, that he has made friends with the tanker driver and, two, that the driver gives him some milk on a regular basis.

That's very much how it goes: if the tanker arrives when you are about, you see the driver every day. For about ten years we were first pick-up in the morning. They weren't allowed to collect the milk before 8am but most days they would reverse up to the dairy at 7.30. Most drivers would sit in the lorry and read the paper until you were ready but the one driver would pour you a cup of tea from his flask and bring it into the parlour whilst you finished milking. Whilst the cup of tea was welcome, for reasons I couldn't detect, the cows didn't like him. When a cow doesn't like something she usually defecates. Although I enjoyed the tea I had a lot more work clearing up afterwards! Defecate is not a word we use a lot on farms.

When we first went from churns to bulk tanks our milk was collected by a large ungainly articulated tanker. At the first sign of snow we had to pull it up to the yard with tractors and as it had to park across the slope to get the milk, it would often bend in the middle on the snow and do a sort of stationary jack knife. Then we had to pull it out again before it could go on its way.

The driver became a good friend and because he came at nine in the morning, which is my breakfast time, he had a breakfast as well. He was big into horse and dog racing and used to give Ann some really good tips. The local bookies used to dread her phone calls! He was friendly with three well-to-do businessmen who lived near him and three nights a week used to drive them hundreds of miles to greyhound racing. I used to reckon that he didn't go to bed three nights a week. He was never late with the lorry and was always immaculately turned out. Goodness knows how he did it.

He was a very good natured man and only had one moan in life. Further on, on his route, he had to go to a farm that had a sort of square farmyard. 'I could easily drive into the yard and turn the lorry around in one go, except for one thing. He's got a workshop on one side of the square and outside the workshop is an anvil. If the anvil wasn't there I could get around in one go. As it is, I have to do a lot of shunting about.' But help is at hand.

His relief driver was a mountain of a man. He was less than six feet tall, but he looked about six feet across the shoulders. His arms were like tree trunks, a slim waist and some more tree trunks for legs. He had the sort of physique that you only see in weight lifters on TV. And he was hard with it. He goes to the farm which has the anvil one day, and whilst he and the farmer are watching the milk go out of the tank he says to the farmer, 'If you were to move that anvil, I could get around in one lock.' The farmer, who has probably had similar requests before, is a bit miffed and says, 'If you can move it, you can have it.'

Without a word the driver goes to his lorry, opens the door of the passenger side, goes to the anvil, picks it up, carries it to the lorry and puts the anvil on the cab floor. He doesn't say a word. Neither does the farmer.

9 SEPTEMBER 2017

It's a busy time for gamekeepers. They have their pheasant poults in what they call release pens. The poults are put in these large pens which they have erected strategically in woods. The idea is that whilst within these pens, the young pheasants are safe from predators. As they grow, they learn to fly out and enjoy a wider world full of food, insects and nature's autumn bounty. They can get back into the pens and safety at night through a sort of one-way system of holes in the fence. There is a low-level electric fence to stop Mr and Mrs Fox following them through the hole.

As the poults get older, they accumulate into large packs, and to the consternation of the keepers, roam considerable distances. These peregrinations (I've been looking to use that word for a long time, it is on a notice board at our local stately home, it means wandering about), usually take them onto a highway, which they seem to enjoy. I've seen vehicles drive right through these packs of young pheasants, without so much as a touch of the brakes, leaving dozens of dead and dying in their wake.

There is a quiet lane down through a very dark wood. It's a bit like the Wild Wood in *Wind in the Willows*, probably full of weasels and ne'er-do-wells. At about 11 in the morning the sun is shining directly down this lane and pheasant poults come out of the woods at each side, to sun themselves.

Last time I went down there the road was full of pheasants. There were hundreds of them and there was no obvious way through. I was in no particular hurry, so I stopped. They surrounded the truck and I could hear them pecking at it. The parking sensors around the truck were going mad and I thought they would surely blow a fuse. The dog Gomer is up on the dashboard going berserk. He would like nothing better than to get into a release pen for an hour to teach these poults how to fly. I've told the keeper that I put him in the pens twice a day and he gives me the thinnest of smiles.

★★★

Aerosol spray markers for sheep and cattle are designed to last for some time. If you have a bunch of cattle or sheep and you want, for management reasons, to identify some within that bunch, you put a coloured spray mark on those you will wish to identify at a later date. A classic example of this would be when your sheep are being scanned to see how many lambs they are carrying. Single lambs, twins or three or four lambs and barren ewes will be marked differently. It will be relatively easy, at a later date, to sort them out into different groups. The very last thing you want is for these spray marks to fade away after a week or so. If you should be marking lambs for example in the summer and you are holding a lamb and the person with the aerosol marker is not concentrating and he sprays your hair red, I wonder how long the red will last?

23 SEPTEMBER 2017

In my experience most farms secretaries took up the role because they were encouraged by their mothers. They were encouraged by their mothers because the mothers thought that it would give their daughters a good chance of marrying a farmer. It could be a classic case of, 'Mother knows best', because in lots of cases their wish came true. But did those mothers know what sort of life those daughters would have? I doubt it.

It would be a life of hard work. Mostly there is a big farm house to run plus milking to do when the men are busy with harvest or silage. There's relief tractor driving to do and everyone knows that rearing calves is women's work. I could go on and on with the list of roles that women perform on farms, the list is endless, and they have nothing but my admiration. Their social life is often poor. A bank manager once told me that he called to see a client, who kept a lot of sheep. They were dipping sheep and the husband was catching the sheep and putting them in the dipping bath and his wife was on the paddle. A paddle is a broom-shaped wooden device with which you push the sheep under the surface of the bath as they swim out. This ensures that the sheep are fully immersed in the dip, so that it is effective. I was told that the wife had a 12-month-old child on a sling on her back and that she was visible heavily pregnant. Childbearing is something the farmer's wife is expected to take in her stride. If she is lucky she will get a week's holiday but there's a 50/50 chance her husband will not have time to go with her.

She will probably get to only about two social functions a year, only a couple of chances to wear a frock. And when she does get a chance to wear a frock, she has to sit down all evening, lest people should see the red welly marks on the back of her legs. All this is down to her mother who started her down this road in the first place.

Her mother would have been very determined in her efforts to get her to marry a farmer. If, for example, the girl came home with a sensible boyfriend, with a sensible 9 till 5 job, driving a sensible car that was kept clean and tidy, the mother would be polite but cool. If on the other hand, the daughter brought home a farmer, the mother would get out the red carpet for him. It wouldn't matter at all that the farmer left footmarks all over that carpet. It would be best not to ask what those footmarks comprised of. Never mind that he was always late picking her up, never mind that he picked her up in a filthy Land Rover. Never mind that the only things she had ever seen that were as filthy and covered in muck as the Land Rover were his hands. Never mind that if you cleaned the filth from out of his fingernails there would be enough for you to put it in a plastic bag and grow tomatoes. Never mind that the mother suspected (quite correctly), that the farmer would direct most of his efforts during the evening, to getting her daughter in the back of his Land Rover. It goes without saying that there was either a dead sheep or calf in the back already.

I've just reread this and it could be that it could be interpreted as not politically correct and sexist. I'm not a bit bothered about PC. That particular pendulum has swung way too far past what is common sense and reasonable. I don't feel it is sexist because during my life I've met hundreds and hundreds of farming families at dinners and shows and all those little stories have been told to me by farmers' wives, and they have all been told me with a laugh and a smile at the irony of it all. In fact some farmers' wives have told me about their regular workload and I've looked at their husbands and wondered what they actually do. There are lots and lots of farmers' wives who do the work of a man and it is the saving of that expense that is often the difference between making the farm viable of not. Never mind the moral support they give.

30 SEPTEMBER 2017

Winding the harvest up to its conclusion is becoming a protracted affair. Very heavy thundery showers have impeded progress. As I write there is still a lot of spring barley and beans to combine. Although it is not complete, dates have been put down for harvest festivals but I suppose you have to put a marker down somewhere. In reality the harvest is never really finished. Maize is harvested in October/November around here and then there's fodder beet and that can drag on all winter and into spring. But autumn is the traditional end to the year's growing cycle and we can't be too picky about dates. It is also the sort of end of the growing cycle for wildlife, so how have they got on?

Some have got on well. I take the dog Gomer up onto my top fields every day. He likes to chase rabbits and there's three of my neighbour's sheep been jumping the fence for months now, he is quite good at getting them to jump back. There were 18 lapwings on the grass. But they weren't any old lapwings. By their size and immature plumage I took them to be this year's hatched lapwings. I've never seen juveniles flock together like this before but that's what they were and that's what they were doing. Just to confirm my sighting, there were eight more lapwings on the next field up that by comparison of size and plumage, were clearly adults. Seeing so many young lapwings about quite buoyed me up.

I needed a bit of good news because I haven't seen a hare for a fortnight now, so it looks as though we have lost that particular battle. I used to see about ten hares a day, any day. I had a text yesterday from the police to look out for a black truck. The truck carries the number plate of a red Discovery, so the police have their work cut out.

Also up on those top fields are large flocks of small birds. I haven't been able to identify them because when they are on the ground you can't see them in the grass and when they fly off they are very quick and you can only see them in silhouette and can't identify their plumage, but there are hundreds of them. If it's the time of year for harvest festivals, then the young lapwings I have seen still in the fields are as much something to celebrate as any basket of apples and tin of baked beans that find their way into a church.

★★★

I know very little about smoking. I tell people I've never smoked but that is not quite true. When I was 16 a friend of mine and I bought ten cigarettes and we smoked them five each in the pictures. I didn't inhale the smoke: it went into the mouth and out through the nose. I had to work to get any money I had and I remember thinking at the time, 'What a waste of money that was.' I've never bought cigarettes since though I do remember scrubbing my fingers for a week in case there were any nicotine stains for my father to see. My wife used to smoke 20 a day. 20 a day is smoker-speak for 40!

One Sunday evening we were watching TV and reading the papers, and she said to me, 'Do you notice anything different about me?' I looked across, scrutinised her and said, 'That new hairstyle really suits you.' 'I haven't had my hair done. I haven't had a cigarette for three days.' And she had stopped, just like that. Since I smoked those five cigarettes, I've had two or three cigars on occasions where I've had too much to drink. I've always regretted it afterwards because I could taste stale cigar for days afterwards!

7 OCTOBER 2017

Those of us ordinary people, that's mostly you and I, could be forgiven for thinking that life in general, and some important issues in particular, are driven by the views of minorities. The trouble is that society at large is so worried at causing offence, as in political correctness, that no one has the courage anymore, to tell someone 'that's a really stupid idea.'

All aspects of life fall into this category but the one that concerns me in particular, and could affect me directly if I live long enough, is the prospect of rewilding. There's plenty of beavers about. Their supporters enthuse about the good they will do. Apparently they will stop flooding, at a stroke. Not that I want to, but should I wish to fell a tree, I would probably need permission, don't think a beaver would bother to ask! Double standards abound!

But of greater concern is the momentum that is gathering towards the reintroduction of lynx. 'They' want to reintroduce lynx to the north of England and the Scottish Borders, to the vast Keilder Forest area. This will be a bit of a test case, the thin end of the wedge. If this is a success the floodgates will open for the reintroduction of other species. Quite what will be considered success is beyond me but you can be sure that those that judge 'success', will be those that do the releasing anyway. My hunch is that the lynx release will go ahead. You can be sure that released lynx will be protected and fitted with trackers so once the cat is out of the bag it will take a lot to put it back in.

Sheep farmers are rightly concerned. But lynx people say that even if they take lambs it doesn't matter because lots of lambs are already lost. Those of us who have been watching the excellent TV programme *This Farming Life* will know that if you have native hill breeds of sheep living in extreme mountain terrain, you will get losses.

I'm not sure how big a lynx is but it is suggested that they will help to control the deer population, which is 'out of hand'. The deer population could be quickly controlled by shooting, the only reason this doesn't happen is because if you shot too many you would crash the price of venison. How long will it be before the lynx work out that sheep and lambs are easier to catch than deer? About two or three weeks.

What else will they eat? You can be sure that they will eat the eggs and young of any ground nesting birds they come across. I don't know why but I associate the wild uplands of the northern border country as being a good place for curlews. Not alongside lynx, it won't be. I don't know if a lynx could outrun a hare but I bet it could ambush one. If you were a leveret you would have no chance.

The proposed reintroduction of the lynx is so important because it will be quickly followed by the reintroduction of the wolf. There are already people waiting in the wings who think this is a good idea. Because wolves are territorial and live in packs and because there is so much food about, they will proliferate and spread far and wide.

Earnest naturalists and gullible *Country File* presenters will sally forth on fine days and give these packs of wolves romantic names. You could have a pack near you. The Gordano pack or the Taunton Deane pack. They will be probably named after motorway services because the wolves will find the motorways very useful to get about their territory. Livestock farmers will have to react by housing sheep and cattle all the year round. Once the wolves have eaten all the wild mammals they can find, and hopefully the odd lynx, you will see them hanging about school playgrounds and care homes. You might think I'm exaggerating but that's how crazy it all is.

One of the so-called 'good' reasons for rewilding is that all these species roamed these islands hundreds of years ago until they were persecuted to extinction. All I can say is that we have managed very well without them thus far, and continue to do so. These islands bear no resemblance to what they did hundreds of years ago. What's the population gone up since then? Three-fold? Ten-fold?

I despair of what our countryside will be like in thirty years' time. All the small songbirds will have disappeared, gone to feed the masses of birds of prey that have proliferated and all the small mammals will have been eaten by species introduced by rewilding. As these predators have no predators themselves, the only limit to their expansion will be the availability of their food source. Don't think that none of this will affect you, because these 'new' animals will soon discover, like foxes have, that there are rich pickings to be had in towns and cities. I think that the prospect to rewild the UK is a really stupid idea.

14 OCTOBER 2017

Did you see *One Man and His Dog* on *Countryfile* recently? I thought the control between shepherd and dog was quite remarkable. It makes those of us less skilled dog owners feel quite humble. The event was staged on Hampstead Heath and the distractions for the dogs were considerable. Not only were there lots of people outside the arena engaged in all sorts of activities, but I thought the dogs, and sheep for that matter, would have been put off by the barking of spectators' dogs. Not a bit of it. Only one young dog was seriously distracted.

★★★

I had a dog, years ago, that would do all that left and right stuff but it took me 12 months to find out. She was a little black bitch called Smut. I bought her at about three years old from a renowned local breeder. He had bred her twice and each time she had carried one large pup that had to be delivered by caesarean section. That couldn't go on, she was spayed and put up for sale. Now that I am reminiscing I recall that if I was in the house, she had a habit of lying on the yard, about 20 yards from the back door. If someone called they would walk warily past her and she wouldn't even lift her head. If she had been depicted, years ago, in a Giles cartoon she would have been just a black blob, with one eye showing. She would wait until the caller had just raised their hand to knock at the door, and she would have slipped noiselessly up behind them and as their hand came down she would give them a sharp nip in the backside. By the time they had realised what had happened and rubbed the affected part she would be away back up the yard, around the corner and out of sight. There would have been no barking, no growling, just a painful bite in the cheek area.

By and large I used to get pleasure out of this biting phenomenon. The pleasure would vary according to how much I liked the caller. Regular callers soon learnt to walk straight in, it was the actual knocking of the door that seemed to be the problem.

At the time I kept about 400 ewes and I used to take Smut to work them. We would go into the field and she would see the sheep and go down into a sort of half crouched position and look at me. She would be like a coiled spring just waiting to be set off. I would say, 'come by' and nothing would happen. Over the coming months she started to work but it was only because she had worked out what we were trying to do. If you keep sheep in the same fields you tend to do the same things with them. You move them about those fields on a regular basis, you get them into the same pens. An intelligent dog soon works it all out. Smut worked it out and started to help. It's different if you keep sheep on an open hill, almost anything can happen, and usually does.

But all the time I knew that there was something that I was missing. I'd had Smut 12 months and there were sheepdog training classes advertised. I took her along. There were ten others there with dogs at a field that was laid out with the pen and gates of a trial. One by one the handlers took their dogs out to the instructor but they were all goodish farm dogs and not trialists and the course was beyond them. I was the last one. 'Tell me about your dog, Roger.' I told the story about us I've told you. I didn't mention the biting. 'I know where this bitch came from, you can't get her to work because she's Welsh speaking. Mind if I have a go?' And he put the sheep through the gates and into the pen as easy as you like, and there was a round of applause from the spectators. Smut and I never looked back.

Gomer the dog was very taken with *One Man and His Dog* – he watched it all, but he was much more interested in a piece I was watching about Siberian huskies.

To conclude, two more doggy stories, no happy ending this week. There's a farmer not far from here keeps a lot of sheep on an open hill. He has a reputation for having the very best of dogs. He goes into his small local town to get some sheep wormer. His

Land Rover is stolen along with his four dogs in the back. He will wonder what happened to those dogs for the rest of your life. I've heard of trucks and dogs being stolen before. People say that the dogs are dumped in cities and left to fend for themselves but of course you don't know that. It's about as sad as it comes. Just look at your dog and imagine it happening to them.

And Smut? We had about six years living and working together. She was my shadow, my constant companion. One day I walked down to the main road to post a letter. Smut was starting to get a bit deaf. I stop at the post box that is in a wall. Smut goes a bit further to see what's about. What's about is a big lorry, going very fast and clipping the verge at the corner. It fatally clipped Smut.

28 OCTOBER 2017

Every day I drive around our fields, always have done. I'm out looking at crops and stock. Just lately I've been looking for hares. Two to three years ago I would see about ten hares as I drove around the fields, ten or twenty hares were a customary part of the journey, these days I drive around the fields in a pattern that will cover all the fields comprehensively, and I haven't seen a hare for three weeks. They have either been driven off or destroyed by the activities of hare coursers. In theory, no hares should mean no hare coursers, but their legacy lives on.

One Sunday morning, at about 8 o'clock, we get a phone call that tells us that we have 40 dry cows and in-calf heifers out on the road, about a mile from where they should be. Cattle usually get out for two reasons. Either they don't have enough to eat in the field where they are supposed to be, or the fences are not good enough. A lightning appraisal of their circumstances tells me that they have plenty of grass, they had only been in the field a week, and the fences were good. We walked them back quite easily, they were very content, they would be, they had been grazing the road side all night. They had got out because the gates into the field were wide open and in the soft ground of the gateway you could easily see the wheel marks where hare coursers had driven in.

That there are members of society who feel free to go onto land and destroy an inoffensive animal like the hare and in so doing let a large group of cattle onto the road without regard for their safety and the safety of other road users, well, it has the feel of anarchy about it.

★★★

In the pub, we are talking about electricity. For once there is a consensus. We are all agreed we are afraid of it and therefore it should be treated with respect. We think that the best place for electricity is down a cable with plenty of insulation around it and it should never be allowed to stray out of its proper environment. Someone says he knows a person who when he is using an extension cable, for welding for example, and the fuse in the plug keeps blowing, thinks nothing of replacing the fuse with a piece of metal he has cut out of a six inch nail. We all know someone like that and we reflect on it quietly.

The subject of electricity had come up because someone had told the story of a farmer who had one of these big self-propelled sprayers. The spray booms on these machines are very long and they are folded and unfolded by hydraulic power. This farmer had been unfolding the booms and not noticed he was under some electricity cables. There was a flash and a bang, the electricity had shorted out through the sprayer and burst all the tyres. The dilemma for the farmer was whether it was safe to get off his immobilised machine. He used his mobile phone to call the police who in turn phoned the power provider in the area, who cut it all off. Mobile phones are invaluable on farms.

I had a sort of similar experience many years ago. My loader had broken down and I had borrowed a neighbour's to put silage out for the cows. It was a tractor with a loader on the front, the only difference was it had a sort of digger on the back. It was a scaled-down version of the digger on the back of a JCB, a 'working man's digger'. The only other difference was, when it was being transported about, it was a lot higher than the cab of the tractor. As I drove it into the yard I pulled the power cables down. I had the same dilemma as the man on the sprayer: is it safe to get off?

But I didn't get where I am today without being resourceful. The wires were down just outside the dairy. Just outside the dairy was a large dish where we gave the cats some milk twice a day. Some cats didn't go far away all day but were within earshot, hiding in adjacent buildings. It was raining quite hard and electricity likes wet. I called out, 'Puss, puss, puss.' Several cats emerged picking their way, delicately, through the wet mud. There was no flash, no bang, no dead cats. They had answered my question for me.

11 November 2017

Over the years, when I have often been short of fresh grazing for the cows, I have cast envious eyes over the grass that grows on the side of the road and wished that I could graze it. It's not a new phenomenon. Many years ago, before traffic was so plentiful and so fast, people would use this road grass. The practice even had a name. It was called 'grazing the long meadow'. Get it? They tell me that in the Second World War, when food was scarce, wider verges were ploughed and potatoes were grown there. When I first came to live around here, the verges were cut using what was then a conventional mowing machine. The proper description is a reciprocating knife – you only see these on combines these days – and these mowers would cut the grass off at the base but otherwise leave it intact.

There was a lady who had a smallholding a few miles away and if the weather was good she would go around and turn this cut grass by hand about two days after it was cut and if the weather was still dry she would cart it home as hay. It was taken home as loose hay and in years where the weather cooperated, she would make all the fodder she needed, in this way. She couldn't do that sort of harvesting today because the verges are cut with flail machines that chop all the grass up and she couldn't feed it to stock anyway because roadside verges are full of polystyrene food trays, plastic bottles and plastic bags. Not all the plastic ends up in the sea. The last time I saw someone grazing the 'long meadow' was on a lane in the west of Ireland about 20 years ago. Two raggedy little boys, barefoot and with the arse out of their trousers, were supervising about 20 cows and calves as they grazed the side of the road.

Roadside verges are one of the great missed opportunities of our time. Narrow strips of verge have to be cut for safety reasons. But there are thousands and thousands of acres of verge on the sides of busy dual carriageways and motorways that could be sown down to nectar-rich flower meadows. Conservationists are forever criticising farmers because wild flower meadows have largely disappeared. Farmers are a small minority in society and easily picked on. They should look to themselves and the rest of society. Society at large own all the roads and all the motorways. Why not put all this vast area to good use and give insects a boost at the same time?

Years and years ago, I used to go quite regularly to France and was always taken with their practice of planting a sort of wild rose down the central reservations between carriageways. How pretty it all looked when the roses were in flower. We seem quite content to fill our central carriageways with weeds and the litter that is, or so it seems, a part of modern life. Proof, if it were needed, that all this works in an ecological sense, are the mile after mile (or should that be kilometre after kilometre) of buzzards that are seen sitting on fence posts alongside the roads in France. The buzzards are there because there is a flourishing population of small mammals present and that in itself is proof that it is all 'working'.

★★★

The last bank has just closed in one of our two local towns. The population is 2,299 so you would think it could support one bank. They promised to keep the cashpoint open for six months but I've been there three time for cash and each time I've come away empty handed. The population is 2,300 when I'm at the cashpoint. There was an open letter on Facebook or Twitter telling the bank that they had reneged on this cashpoint promise but I particularly liked the bit at the end of the message. 'Presumably you closed this bank to save money – did you know you've left the lights on?'

18 NOVEMBER 2017

I've got these five grandchildren. Five is enough. There was a time when they could all get on my lap at the same time. I used to say, 'Get off, I don't like children.' Then they'd say, 'Oh yes you do.' They are all growing up now and well past the lap-sitting stage. The eldest boy works on the farm now and he also has a girlfriend, which was to be expected. But the girlfriend has brought her horse here! There's lots of issues with horses but the main one seems to be that they are always eating. She says 'Do you want to come and see it?' I told her I'd sit in my armchair and I expected that it would run past the window before long. There's a story about when people were training to be salespersons to call on farms.

They were told that if they went to a farm for the first time and they saw one horse there, that was OK. If there were three horses there, to be careful. If there were five or more there, to turn the car around and drive back out. That, to me, quite neatly sums up the financial benefits of keeping horses.

When my own children were small I bought them two Welsh section A foals that had come off the mountain that morning. To be fair it was me that wanted the ponies rather than the children. I broke them in myself, after a fashion, but it didn't really work. I was young and busy and didn't really have the time to spend with them that they needed. It always took a long time to catch them and they were so much trouble that when you had caught them, you wished you hadn't. We had more B&B in those days and children were always wanting to ride them. We had an accident here one day so I decided the ponies would have to go. No one wanted to buy them so I swapped them for two donkeys. The donkeys were in foal and one thing lead to another and after two or four years we had five donkeys. Wish I had five donkeys now, they seem to be worth a bit of money. The last time we had donkeys here I had two seaside donkeys for the winter for the grandchildren to ride. You couldn't ride them far: after 50 yards they wanted to turn back.

25 November 2017

The stream that runs down the length of the main street of our village has been just a trickle for most of the year, as have been most watercourses in the area. But recent rains have brought it back to life and with the extra flow have come brown trout. There is a special interest in these, especially if there is a 'big' one amongst them. There is talk of catching them by tickling them but the most successful catchers are housewives armed with toasting forks.

2 December 2017

Our Christmas tree went up on 1st December. After that things quickly get out of hand. One of the things that was getting out of hand was my Christmas card list. I decided a few years ago to stop sending any and to send the money to charity. This year I've sent it to Children in Need. I have no problem in saying that some of the stories make me cry. Years and years ago I was telling my daughter that I had shed a tear. 'There's no problem in a man these days crying at a sad story.' Thirty year later this man still gets a bit moist around the eyes and now he is not afraid to admit it. There are stories about children whose bravery is an example to us all and whose situations in life put our own lives in perspective.

The other thing that is getting out of hand is Christmas presents. As grandchildren get older it is difficult to get them something worthwhile. I've done all my Christmas shopping and I've done next year's as well. I give them all money. But that solution gets serious. My son reckons that we should all give each other a fiver, that we should all spend it in charity shops, and we will see who gets the best bargain. Whichever way you look at it, the idea has much to commend it. There's a cap on what you spend and all the money goes to charity. I quite like it.

★★★

My wife had let the dog Gomer out for a comfort break and he had been gone for two hours and when he came back he was covered with mud and exhausted. We wondered where he had been.

I found out at the pub on Sunday night. I let the local shoot walk over our land. We get a few pheasants hanging about in the trees that screen our chicken sheds and that is not the best biosecurity, so it's just as well the shoot goes through there before they get too settled. Seems that Gomer's ablution requirements had coincided with the arrival of the shoot, and he had joined them for the two hours. He had even jumped into the beaters' cart when they had moved on to their next drive.

It was the first time for some to see him and they were all very taken with him, as are most people who meet him.

I get these enquiries in the pub on Sunday night. 'That terrier of yours, is he any good down a foxhole?' I've not done that with him. I've thought that he would be a good ratter but I'm frightened he will get stuck in the bales.

★★★

It's been a slow start to this year's shooting stories but at last here is one. On the ground they shoot over, there is a crop of mustard that has grown away, probably because of the mild weather, and is now in flower. It is intended to be ploughed in as a sort of green manure. It's very dense and is bound to harbour some pheasants. They decide to put three beaters and three dogs through it. In fact there were four dogs, because by now Gomer had joined the shoot. But it wasn't quite that simple. The mustard was over head height, well over head height. It was in a block of 45 acres in a field that didn't have any trees in it. When the three beaters had gone about a 100 yards they were well and truly lost. The only things they could see to guide them were the clouds. Clouds as landmarks are notoriously unreliable. It sounds a bit funny now but they were soaked to the skin, even their hats were wet, and the only way they could get out was by putting their sticks up in the air and waving to the guns, who stood on their trucks and directed them out by shouting. 'Your dog was in there with us, didn't think we'd ever see him again,' says one. My dog is made of sterner stuff. He's in love this week, but that's another story.

16 DECEMBER 2017

Today we consider vegetables. As Christmas bears down on us I feel it should be a discussion about sprouts, but it's not, it's cauliflower. Not the cauliflower that you might grow in your garden or allotment, but cauliflower that is grown professionally and commercially. My first cauli story was told to me about ten years ago. The grower was visibly upset by it all, he seemed a genuine man and very believable. He had a contract to supply cauli to a major supermarket and was to deliver them to a proper packing station. They were to be packed 12 in a box and after they were put in the box they were covered with a sheet of cling film. Off they went down a conveyor. If one or more of the caulis were a bit bigger than the others and touching the cling film, the whole box was rejected.

The grower sees this going on and says he will put staff in there and they will take the offending box, remove the offending cauli, put a smaller one in, replace the cling film, and put the box back on the line. He is refused permission to do this as 'It will be disruptive to our procedures and protocols,' so the rejected boxes, cardboard and vegetables, go to the shredder together and are sent to landfill! But our grower is appalled by the waste of it all and says he will put staff on the line to intercept the rejected boxes and he will take it all home and feed the cauli to his cattle. 'You can't do that it will disrupt etc.' Well, you know the rest.

★★★

My second story is more recent, in fact, it's current. This cauli grower has his own packing facility. He does all the packing himself and sends all the produce to the supermarket distribution centre. Part of the packing process is for him to put the end price on, which is 65p. He is getting 15p. Pause awhile and think about that. He has to grow, with all that entails, harvest, pack and transport for his 15p. But it gets worse. Should any of the cauliflowers get rejected on their journey from distribution centre to shopper's trolley, for whatever reason, it could be shape, a blemish or even a shopper dropping it on the floor, the grower pays for that. And not the 15p he has been paid but the 65p that is the end price! If he gets one rejected he has to sell more than four to pay for it. And he's already had the cost of production.

You might reasonably ask, how does he ever make a profit? He probably just makes enough to think he'll grow some more next year. Which is how it all works. If he complains too much they won't want him to grow them any more vegetables anyway. Which is also how it works. They will sign up another grower instead, and he for his part will be delighted to have landed a supermarket contract. Delight that will last just as long as it takes for reality to kick in. I've had very similar stories relating to experiences I have had in the dairy industry. But although I don't like Christmas very much, I've no great wish to spend it in prison.

23 December 2017

What's the worst Christmas I can remember? It started off OK. We had friends and their little boy to stay. We decided, the father and I, to go to the pub 'for an hour,' on Christmas Eve. 'You mind you are back by nine, the children will be in bed and you can carry these presents upstairs.' Well you know how it is, there's a really good atmosphere in the pub on Christmas Eve. Eleven o'clock comes and news comes in that a pub about two miles away has an extension so, carried away by the euphoria of it all, we decide to try just one drink at the other pub. One thing leads to another (as it often does), and we get home at 2am. Boy, were they nasty! They were so nasty I still remember it well.

But there's worse to come. We deserved the Christmas Eve 'nasty' but I didn't see the need to be so nasty the next day. We are harking back to the days before satellite television. There's a mast on a high hill, up next to where my hares used to be. To get a picture on our TV you had to be able to see the mast and your aerial had to point at it. Our aerial had moved in the night. Naturally, this was my fault for being late home. The children had opened their presents and now wanted to watch TV. I need to explain, ours is a two storey house and there's only one place you can get on the roof, there's a sort of gulley in the roof. The trouble is that this gulley is directly above the steps that go down to the cellar, so when you get up a ladder you are looking down the equivalent of four floors. We had to join three ladders together to get up and there was about five feet of 'give' where the ladders joined. I am terrible at heights, as we shall see, but the scary climb of the ladder was to be preferred to the alternative of two nasty women standing at the bottom. We moved the aerial and got the picture back and a sort of peace was restored.

This fear of heights is something I've had all my life. Three of us went to Sydney for the 2003 Rugby World Cup. The other two did all the organising and the first morning there they organised a walk over the harbour bridge. They did this confident that I wouldn't do it. There's quite an induction process involved before you go, they even breathalyse you, and all the time that was going on I was wondering how I could escape. I knew that if I 'bottled it', I would never be allowed to forget it. Then I saw a group of old granny's coming off the bridge and thought – if they can do it, so can I. I did it! Now whenever that bridge is shown on TV, and it often is, I always say to the family, 'I've walked over that.' That will do me for heights. If I am asked to climb a ladder I decline, with the qualification that 'I've walked over Sydney harbour bridge.'

That afternoon we decided we would go for a boat tour of the harbour. My two friends went to get the tickets and I sat on a bench in the sun. It was close to the Opera House on what I think they call Circular Quay. I put my head back and closed my eyes and soaked up the sun. Then I get a sharp elbow in the ribs. I have a look and it's a dairy farmer I know from Ayrshire. I used to be chairman of a large dairy cooperative and he had been at a meeting I had chaired in Scotland five days previously, he had given me a hard time about the milk price we were paying. There was no 'Hello, fancy seeing you here.' What he said was, 'How can you afford to come out here on the price you are paying for milk?' I said, 'You are getting the same price as me, and you can afford it!' That was it, off he went. On the boat later, my friends said they were so proud of me for walking the bridge they would treat me to dinner. They booked a table at a restaurant at the very top of Sydney's highest building. The lift up there was one of those plastic bubbles on the outside of the building!

I had a ticket for the World Cup final but I didn't go. I reasoned that if England won I would hear about it for the rest of my life, so why would I want to watch then do it as well? I sold the ticket and spent the money around the bars and restaurants of Darling Harbour. It was one of the better judgement calls I have made in my life.

★★★

I worked every Christmas day for nearly 60 years – most livestock farmers are the same. I didn't mind that so much, what I used to mind were the people who worked in other industries asking how much time I had off over Christmas. They all seemed to get close to a week. It annoyed me that they didn't realise that farms were a 24/7 operation long before 24/7 was a concept. I can't work any more and the irony is that if I could choose any Christmas present I wanted, it would to be well enough to work.

30 DECEMBER 2017

We were reminiscing in the pub. Have you noticed how most of my stories have a 'once upon a time' feel to them? What started us off was the news that the pub had resurrected a darts team. Thirty years ago the same pub had two or three darts teams, two or three domino teams, a pool team and, in the summer, two tug-of-war teams. I used to pull tug-of-war, I was never any good at darts and I didn't like dominoes. It's too noisy when they shuffle them and I don't enjoy the interminable post mortems after each hand. All that was when most of the local residents were working people; today most local people are retired newcomers.

Once a year the landlord of the pub would put on a dance in the village hall. You could only go if you were in one of the teams. There was free food and free drink all night and I've started a headache just thinking about it.

As you go through the front door of the pub there is a table in the window and it was used to play dominoes all night long. There would be four people playing and most people who came through the front door would knock the domino table with their knuckles. This was called 'putting a knock on.' What it meant was that that person wanted to join the queue of those waiting for a game. The two players who had just lost the game would be replaced by two who had 'got a knock on', and so it would continue all night. Sometimes, strangers would come in, mostly early on in the evening, and sit drinking at the domino table. The regular players would stand about glaring at them until they moved. There were plenty of other tables in the pub but they would only use that one. This always intrigued me because they were quite happy to use the other tables on Fridays when there were matches against other pubs. When the strangers showed signs that they were going, they were almost jostled out of their seats so that the domino players could make a start.

If you went out of the room where the domino table is, you go through a wide arch into the second room. There's about three feet of wall on your left as you enter the second room, it probably holds the pub up. The dartboard used to be on this bit of wall. One night there was a darts match on and one of the visiting players missed the dartboard, missed the wall and the dart went another ten or 12 feet and stuck in the head of a domino player. Fortunately it was only his dignity that was hurt.

This man was a bit of a character. One night he had walked the two miles to the pub and at about 11.30pm he tried to get a lift home with a young man who lived near him who had a powerful motorbike. The driver was adamant that he wouldn't give him a lift as he didn't have a spare helmet with him. Unfortunately there was more drink about than common sense and it was decided that the landlord would lend him a galvanised bucket to wear on his head with the handle under his chin.

Thus they set off. The motorbike owner only knew one speed – fast. Before they had got out of the village the bucket had slipped off his passenger's head and the handle was around his neck. They were going so fast that the force of the wind in the bucket put so much pressure on the handle that it threatened to choke him. Whether it's a good thing or a bad thing that things like that don't happen today, depends on your point of view.